D0868431

PRAISE FOR
Journeys with Jimmy
and Other Adventures in Media

"*Journeys with Jimmy Carter* is a heartfelt and beautifully written memoir about life in the fast lane of American journalism and politics. Barry Jagoda's storytelling about his producer years at CBS and NBC News is fantastic. His delineation on how reporting has changed for the 20th to the 21st century is eye opening and prescient. Highly recommended!"

> —**Douglas Brinkley**, Katherine Tsanoff Brown Chair in Humanities and Professor of History at Rice University, Author of *Cronkite* and *The Unfinished Presidency*, among others

"Barry Jagoda's memoir is timely: in the course of relating his insider's experiences working in the White House of President Jimmy Carter, it vividly reminds us that a position of high office does not have to preclude competence and principled behavior."

> —**Elizabeth Blackburn**, Nobel Laureate in Physiology or Medicine; President Emerita, Salk Institute; Professor Emerita, Biochemistry and Biophysics, University of California, San Francisco

"Journalists, real journalists, are a special breed. They find facts hidden in lies. They tell us who our leaders really are. They risk character assassination and literal assassination to inform readers. Barry Jagoda's life story, told here through personal memoire and riveting anecdote, is a stark warning. We had in Jimmy Carter an honest and intelligent president. We have the antithesis in the White House now. Jagoda tells us why and what we can do to fight back."

> —**Frank Ochberg MD**, Former Associate Director, the National Institute of Mental Health Editor, Post-traumatic Therapy and Victims of Violence

"Presidencies all have their own unique stories. Working in the White House advising the world's most powerful leader can be exhilarating, infuriating, addictive, troubling, useful, and harmful. There are few who have experienced those episodes as an insider. Barry Jagoda is both a scholar and practitioner of media and politics. His experience and insight offer a unique view into Jimmy Carter's presidency told like no other."

—**CYRUS KROHN**, Former Publisher of *Slate Magazine*, worked for Presidents George H. W. and George W. Bush

"Barry Jagoda combines interesting insights into the news operations of America's TV networks in the pre-cable days with a lively, personality-filled account of how his own ambition and experiences landed him a job as a key media adviser in President Carter's White House. His description of the power struggle there shows how his support for spotlighting Carter's agenda of multiple policy goals clashed with the effort by political advisers to present a more focused media message, a perennial conflict in many presidencies. In all, a fascinating picture of some enduring aspects of life in the White House."

—**CARL P. LEUBSDORF**, Former Washington Correspondent, Reporter for *The Baltimore Sun*, Writer for *The Dallas Morning News*

"As we are living through a time when truth isn't truth anymore, with Barry Jagoda's insider and brilliantly insightful analysis, we see the burdens and ultimate moral triumph of the Jimmy Carter presidency. An antidote for Trump-era ennui and a game plan for the 2020 election."

—**PAUL WILKES**, Author of *Six American Families*; *In Due Season: A Catholic Life*; *Your Last Chapter: Creating a Meaningful Life on Your Own Terms*, among others

"Readers of a certain age will love Jagoda's insightful walk down memory lane. He was present at many of the events that shaped our lives. His vivid recollections will help us remember who we are and where we were."

—**DAVID ROSENBLOOM**, Political Scientist at Boston University School of Public Health, Former Commissioner of Health and Hospitals in Boston

"This book is essential reading for anyone who wants an inside view of journalism and politics. Barry Jagoda comes from the tradition of superb journalism that was developed by Edward R. Murrow and Walter Cronkite. We need journalists like Barry Jagoda more than ever."

—**VICTOR EMANUEL**, Ornithologist and Environmentalist, Founder of VENT, Victor Emanuel Nature Tours

"Barry Jagoda has been active in just about every important part of the public's business, and tells about it superbly. *Journeys with Jimmy Carter and Other Adventures in Media* is a lively read, intelligent, insightful—and also fun—throughout."

—**ROBERT E. HUNTER,** Former US Ambassador to NATO, Former Carter Administration National Security Council Director for West European Affairs and Middle East Affairs

Journeys with Jimmy Carter
and Other Adventures in Media

by Barry Jagoda

© Copyright 2020 Barry Jagoda

ISBN 978-1-64663-031-8

All rights reserved. No part of this publication may be reproduced, stored in a retrieval system, or transmitted in any form or by any means—electronic, mechanical, photocopy, recording, or any other—except for brief quotations in printed reviews, without the prior written permission of the author.

Cover Image Courtesy of Carter Library

Published by

210 60th Street
Virginia Beach, VA 23451
800-435-4811
www.koehlerbooks.com

JOURNEYS
WITH
JIMMY CARTER
AND OTHER
ADVENTURES
IN MEDIA

BARRY JAGODA

VIRGINIA BEACH
CAPE CHARLES

To Karen A.B. Jagoda, partner and perennial inspiration:

"If you want to go quickly, go alone.
If you want to go far, go together."

TABLE OF CONTENTS

INTRODUCTION

I n 1975, as the lead television producer for CBS News (and for the group of reporters from all the other American TV networks), I was flying on Air Force One into Soviet East Asia, heading for Vladivostok to lay the news coverage groundwork for the summit meeting between President Gerald Ford and General Secretary Leonid Brezhnev.

The pilot was Colonel Ralph Albertazzie, whose many career highlights in the Cold War included flying President Richard Nixon to China in 1972 for his historic, groundbreaking visit in that country. After inviting me into the cockpit and giving a knowing look, the colonel said, "This is the first time an American military plane has been in these parts without a real threat of being shot down."

Less than two years after that trip, I would give up my exciting job as a top news producer to become television advisor to Jimmy Carter. National exposure was brand new for the previously almost-unknown presidential candidate. In early 1976, Carter, then the former governor of Georgia, had just won the New Hampshire Democratic primary. He and I were about to head by car to the broadcast location of "CBS News with Walter Cronkite," and then for interviews I had set up with the news anchors at NBC News and ABC News.

At the knock of James Wooten, principal politics reporter for *The New York Times*, I rolled down the back window of the sedan. "Governor," exclaimed the normally calm Wooten to Carter, "I think you have just won the Democratic nomination for president."

Carter looked up from his briefing papers and said, "Thanks, Jim. Good deal."

With that, we were off to the first of many encounters over several months with the television networks, doing interviews that would help pave the way for the previously unknown "Jimmy Who" to become the 39th occupant of the White House.

As Carter's television advisor, I was in for the adventure of a lifetime, which continued when I was named special assistant to the president in the White House. In Carter I saw a man of dignity, character and understatement, a man who put country before self, even at his own peril.

By 1980, I had gone on from the White House and was experiencing a Washington, DC that was hostile to those of us who had been Carter partisans. But now I had a spectacular idea: I had by then married DC think-tank policy analyst Karen Bernhardt, and we decided to become bicoastal, acquiring the movie rights to a sentimental and delightful novel, *The Man Who Brought the Dodgers Back to Brooklyn*. We would move to Los Angeles to make this story into a blockbuster movie.

Still, we maintained our base in the nation's capital, where we eventually returned, and where I was to begin a new career in marketing, employing traditional and emerging new media. At first, I became a director at George Washington University, and then was a publicist for Canada's largest technology company. I went on to become Washington director for a worldwide productivity firm and, eventually, returned to a satisfying stint as a reporter and writer in print journalism. Finally, when I accepted an assignment as director of communications at the University of California in San Diego (UCSD), my wife, Karen, and I moved there permanently.

This last job provided two world-class advantages—the splendid weather in San Diego's La Jolla beach community, and, professionally, I now had gratifying work helping scholars focused on significant research.

As you will see, this story—my story—of an American journey in media and politics is set in the context of a political coming of age during the Vietnam period. We all were living analog lives then—we still used mainly traditional means of political communication. A leader might make pronouncements, but those could mostly soon be overtaken by an extremely diligent and wary news media.

It was because of an almost worshipful respect for the First Amendment, fearing the perils of distortions of the political process, that I had chosen journalism as a way of telling truth to power. But after what had been an unforgettably meaningful and very successful career at CBS News and NBC News, I was now categorized as a political operative, and the doors of journalism seemed closed to me. One might have thought that White House name recognition was bound to open doors in Hollywood. But after a year of explorations there, I realized that marketing and digging deep to learn to use the emerging new media seemed the best path for this former crusader.

My first new career direction was in higher education promotion, followed by a decade in high technology public relations. I was pleased that these assignments were lucrative. They both gave me opportunities to really help my faculty clients, and to share my experience with executives pushing the envelope, particularly in telecommunications. My work could never have been successfully accomplished without a strong grounding in the old, legacy media.

I had transitioned from being a legacy, or traditional, media practitioner to becoming a new media expert. In fact, I was almost embarrassed to become characterized as one of the globe's leading authorities in the use of the legacy media, and also in new ways of communicating using what became known as digital and social media.

I was getting surprisingly soulful returns—and learning a lot—in this mostly commercial work.

Returning to journalism, engaging in worldwide travel and writing, turned out to be even more to my liking. Although work as a travel and political writer was strenuous, it was also greatly enjoyable. But being away from home was very tough on family life and not the best way to financially help sustain Karen and me back in DC.

What turned out to be an unexpected great benefit was that Karen was bringing home substantial bucks, and getting lots of respect from her commercial and research work in computers, information technology and the internet's new media. In the late 1980s, her employer in computer sales had invited Karen to a highest performers conference. The firm was celebrating its best salespeople with a trip to San Diego. So my loving spouse brought me along to get in some golf and to hang around at a world-class spa.

As I ended my holiday there, deeply appreciating the weather, I asked Karen, "Honey, why are we not living here?" This beautiful and practical woman looked me in the eye and jokingly said, "We are not living in this climate because you don't have a job here!" She was right, of course, as she has been so often in our forty-two years of partnership and marriage.

So, many years later—when the opportunity arose—I joined the ranks of higher education boosters, this time in the incomparably excellent environment of coastal San Diego. This assignment turned out well for my new employer, The University of California, and for me as well and, eventually, for my longtime devoted spouse. I served nearly a decade working at what had become the highly regarded UCSD, often thought of as the nation's best young university. But now, in semi-retirement, a window finally opened for me to write this story, providing time to think back to roots, and rising to remember and memorialize some dear friends and family.

As we approach the 2020 presidential election, I cannot help but measure the high-mindedness of the noble political leader I served in the White House, and many others in the media or academia, against the manipulative methods and nefarious motives of the man occupying the Oval Office—a man who became only the fourth American president to be impeached. As a nation, we are now on an important journey as we face the crucial democratic challenge to rid our country of the villainous Donald Trump.

Ironically, Trump intuitively knew that the battlefield for his re-election would come through his devious use of the new media. And he also possesses the megaphone that comes with presidential incumbency.

In the case of Jimmy Carter, those media extensions were mostly for the good of our people. Now, Trump, continuously addicted to lying, is summed up in one word—evil. Trump's own dishonest use of media is now a fundamental threat to our daily lives. This is the opposite approach taken by those of us in the Carter Administration.

Approaching the 2020 election, we as a people are faced with a "permanent campaign" from the White House, characterized by daily lies and often-successful efforts to restrict and manipulate the free flow of information. The term "fake news" is now ingrained in our lexicon, further deepening cultural and political schisms dividing this country.

But now every citizen has a chance to make a real difference by paying attention and by developing and implementing a personal media campaign. Each of us can overcome frustration by encouraging turnout of voters who share our views and priorities. A guide for an effective way forward is described Chapter 18.

Now, even in the midst of the worldwide COVID-19 pandemic, I write this memoir after sixty years in the media business, both reporting and making news. I hope my experiences will inform yours, and that come Election Day 2020 we will restore integrity and civility to public life.

PART I

THE CARTER YEARS

CHAPTER 1

CAMPAIGN OF 1976

After an early start to my career in journalism with NBC News, I had become an award-winning producer at CBS News. There we sought to shine a light on politicians: "telling truth to power." But suddenly, at age thirty-two, I found myself right at the very top level of American political power.

This unlikely turn came after the veteran CBS News correspondent Ed Bradley had mentioned my name to Jody Powell, then press secretary to former Georgia Governor Jimmy Carter, who in 1976 was a long-shot candidate for the White House. Trying to get attention, Carter had been going around the country exclaiming, "I'm Jimmy Carter, and I'm running for President of the United States." Bradley, covering this improbable campaign for CBS, told Powell that he knew a guy who could help with his number one problem—Jody Powell knew essentially nothing about national television coverage of presidential elections, much less how to harness it for the campaign's advantage.

After ten years in television news, I was now ready for a new challenge, which my friend Bradley knew. However, when Carter and his people invited me to New Hampshire for a chat, I wasn't sure that working in politics, let alone in their quixotic try for the nation's top office, would in any way be a wise career direction. At that time, I was quite skeptical of Jimmy Carter. I had only met him once, at a conference two years earlier, and he had been rather unimpressive. Now this guy was trying to promote his very long-shot candidacy. And philosophically, I was hesitant to become a booster for any politician.

Eventually, the Carter drama would be another adventure to add to several that had come before it. Already, I had toiled in jobs for the professional football and baseball teams in my hometown of Houston, and had worked in cub reporter positions on two daily newspapers there. I went on to earn a graduate degree in journalism from Columbia University under the critical eyes of Professor Fred Friendly, who, in a dispute over coverage of Vietnam War congressional hearings, had quit as president of CBS News. Friendly had then started up a broadcast program at Columbia's Graduate School of Journalism.

I had worked on a dream to emulate "ping-pong diplomacy" by traveling to Cuba to arrange a major league baseball series between Cuban and American All-Stars. I had covered the Watergate turmoil of Nixon, winning an Emmy Award. And between the Cuba baseball project and Watergate, I had been a Walter Cronkite producer of CBS's coverage of the Apollo moon-landing.

But in a way, my work with the Carter candidacy could be seen as a continuation of the early excitement I had felt when working on projects that were at the top of our country's national agenda.

Coming of age in the Vietnam period and fearing perils of the political process, I had chosen journalism as the way to shine light on the work of politicians. Now, after plaudits and industry awards at CBS News and NBC News, with some success in publicizing governmental antidemocratic practices, I, the once-reluctant political participant, was to join the campaign of Jimmy Carter, eventually serving as an assistant in his White House.

The Carter campaign had made an unexpectedly strong showing in Iowa, and was facing increased coverage in New Hampshire in early

1976. With that came greater scrutiny of Carter's real or perceived weaknesses, including his positions on various issues and his lack of national political identity. Neither Jody Powell, the candidate's principal media advisor, nor Governor Carter himself, knew much about television news coverage beyond what they had experienced in and around Atlanta. They were struggling when Bradley, who had been following the Carter effort, recommended that Powell have a conversation with me.

That made sense; I had skills and insight from my years as a journalist, including a role in coverage of two previous presidential election cycles. In January 1976, Powell and I had an extensive talk at a bar in New Hampshire. His boss, of course, was still a long shot, though he had done well in Iowa. If Carter could somehow continue this kind of showing in the New Hampshire Democratic Presidential Primary, he would have to be taken seriously. My discussion with Powell was positive enough for him to set me up to meet with Governor Carter a few days later.

I had prepared for this encounter by reading Carter's campaign autobiography, *Why Not the Best*, the title of which came from a question Carter had been asked when, as a young naval officer, he had applied for a job with Admiral Hyman Rickover's submarine corps. Besides the reading, I had gone to a few New Hampshire events and observed Carter's passion when he was still pretty much unknown.

Eventually, the candidate found a few minutes to interview me. His first question centered on how I would try to change him or his style.

"Well, Governor," I answered, "I would be letting you know what effect your words will have on the television people, and others, who are covering you."

That was apparently the right answer for this self-assured campaigner. He asked a few more questions and then called Jody over.

"This fellow can probably help us, if he wants to," Carter said. With that, I became a member of the Carter campaign staff.

At the time I wasn't sure if this was a near-hit or a near-miss.

Was I going to waste a few months after leaving CBS, while I tried to develop new entrepreneurial opportunities? Or with Carter, would I be getting somewhere—or nowhere? I decided to give this new adventure a try.

One thing I knew for sure was that if Governor Carter made any kind of decent showing in New Hampshire, he would dominate the national headlines, so my job would be to position him, over the next months, in the most favorable light for television coverage. I was particularly well-qualified to do this back in 1976 when the broadcast news field was still dominated by three main (or "legacy") outlets: CBS News, ABC News and NBC News.

The earliest dramatic moment came with the results on New Hampshire's primary election night, February 24. Carter understood New Hampshire retail politics, and with his "peanut brigade" of supporters, he had won this first big contest.

I knew all the networks would want interviews, and I had spent time researching where their anchors would be on the evening of the primary. Of additional importance, through significant time spent in television news, I had the advantage of knowing and being respected by dozens of network news producers. I had benefited from this same kind of work—organizing coverage—just a few years earlier. The campaign scheduler assigned me to take Carter around that election night.

CBS News Anchor Walter Cronkite with Governor Jimmy Carter

Credit: CBS Photo Archive CBS

As I'd planned, the media coverage of the results was like the crowning of a victorious candidate, propelling him immediately into front-runner status.

The next big race would be the Florida primary and then we would have six more months of hard work ahead.

Carter knew he had to win in Florida. There, it was critical for Carter to beat Alabama Governor George Wallace to show that redneck segregationism would be rejected by the Democrat Party. For this challenge, Carter and campaign manager Hamilton Jordan had assigned a highly trusted and talented young aide, Phil Wise, to direct the Florida effort. Like Carter, Wise had grown up in the tiny south-central Georgia community of Plains. And Phil's hardworking ground operation in Florida prevailed.

The next challenge was in the Midwest. Could the former Southern governor and peanut farmer win in the Rust Belt? The answer, in Wisconsin, turned out to be a decisive yes.

During this period, I was gaining much higher regard for Carter, particularly because of his incisive intelligence and his ability to read crowds. One day, assigned as the staff person to ride with the candidate from speech to speech to provide feedback and handle any problems, I could not help but ask the fifty-one-year-old former governor a question: "I notice that you very often tell your crowds that you and Rosalynn have three sons—but that you and your wife had deliberated for fourteen years before deciding to have Amy. Why this story?"

Carter looked at me with his piercing blue eyes and said, "You're divorced, aren't you?" I nodded yes, wondering how he had picked up that tidbit. But he went on. "So, you might not know that married couples often discuss this subject?" I nodded again. "Telling that true story sets me up in automatic touch with many—perhaps most—in the audience." I just nodded again, wondering at the meaning of what I had just been told.

But the candidate came to trust my instincts and even seemed to value having me around. One late afternoon, as the growing Carter campaign motorcade of a half-dozen cars drove through the streets of Manhattan, we were about to pass my apartment on Madison Avenue.

"Oh, God," I mumbled, "I left my briefcase!"

"Stop the car," ordered Carter. "Go get it, Barry, but be quick." Of course, I ran up three stories while the campaign caravan waited. The moment seemed amusing to some, but later historian Paul F. Boller reported this anecdote, among many others in his 1984 book, *Presidential Campaigns*.

About this time, to prove that Carter was not merely an isolated Bible-thumper, his staff agreed to an interview with the tough-minded liberal reporter Robert Scheer who was writing a profile of Carter for *Playboy* magazine. When the piece appeared, the campaign suffered its greatest threat up to then because it quoted Carter, then widely known as pious Sunday-school teacher, as saying, "I've looked on a lot of women with lust. I've committed adultery in my heart many times."

Reporters, who love to find contradictions in the words and actions of public figures, pounced. We spent the next weeks of the campaign trying to explain away this flagrancy.

Months later, we gathered in San Francisco for one of the presidential debates, and a few of us took Scheer to dinner trying to make up for the controversy that had resulted from his story. It was to be a pleasant evening at a Chinese diner in Oakland. Somehow, the great local columnist Herb Caen found out about the event and attended. We were pleased, expecting a nice story. But the story never materialized, probably because, just as we were leaving the restaurant, some unknown jokester threw a lemon meringue pie all over Caen's beautiful white linen suit.

CHAPTER 2

THE GREAT DEBATES

Though I had now left behind my work as a professional journalist, the skills and insight from ten years in the news business served me well on the Carter campaign. I could see how the combination of a continuously winning candidate, along with interviews by the network news stars—not just by reporters at remote locations—had yielded a sense of inevitability. Carter was being treated as the probable Democratic Party nominee by television news, and even by newspaper and wire-service reporters.

My additional role in the various primary election campaigns, tasks which also suited my previous jobs as a news producer, was to help our increasingly skillful advance persons understand how to best position Carter for live television events that came each Tuesday night. In those days, television news producers set up and coordinated coverage. With my own experience, it was not too difficult to understand how they, along with their correspondents, might react to any given political candidate action.

By the time of the Democratic National Convention, July 12, 1976 in New York's Madison Square Garden, Carter already had more than enough delegates to clinch the nomination. My goal was to get the best arrangements for our candidate, and to make sure he would be comfortable at the podium when delivering his acceptance speech. By now there was no need to coach Carter on delivery or speaking style.

Barry Jagoda, left, and Governor Jimmy Carter at Democratic Convention Podium

Credit: Collection of Barry Jagoda

We knew that the general election campaign would focus on debates with the Republican nominee. My job was to focus on the complex logistics and planning, making sure our candidate was treated fairly. This role produced a near-daily stream of quotes in *The New York Times* and in most of the other national news media. But none of the media attention would be of much value unless Carter was able to adequately prepare for the contest against incumbent President Gerald R. Ford—and emerge victorious.

The audience for the first debate was expected to be huge: in the 1976 election, both nominees had agreed to the historic resumption of presidential campaign debates which had not been held since the famous contests between Richard Nixon and John F. Kennedy in 1960. Now more than 80 million viewers would tune in.

The leading academic authority on presidential debates, Professor Sidney Kraus of Cleveland State University, wrote, "Just as the Kennedy-Nixon confrontations were credited with tipping the balance in favor of the Democratic challenger, the Carter-Ford debates were instrumental in securing Carter's slim margin of victory sixteen years later."

Carter agreed, writing, "The debates were a central element in the 1976 election. As perhaps nothing else could have, they provided an opportunity for the American people to weigh the merits of the candidates. President Ford had come to office only two years before, without a chance to define his views in a national campaign. I had never held national office and was relatively unknown."

Later, former president Ford wrote, "I think the fact that we did debate . . . makes a strong case for their being held in the future." President Ford was right. Face-offs like the '76 debate have now been held every four years as a vital element to presidential elections.

1976 Presidential Debates
Credit: Lori Ferber

Inside the Carter-Mondale campaign, we staffers saw debates as an important chance for our challenger to not only be present on the same stage with the incumbent, but also as an opportunity to show the American people the lightning-quick mind of Jimmy Carter. Though there was the normal apprehension about such highly focused events, the Carter campaign was prepared to win, with the normal confidence we all had in Carter's ability to prevail in such a contest. We welcomed the chance to get on an even field, a level setting with President Ford.

The League of Women Voters, the debate's sponsor, had chosen various sites around the country at locations with historic importance. Philadelphia had been a natural choice for the bicentennial year. San Francisco, site of the signing of the United Nations charter, was selected for the second debate because the subject was to be foreign policy. Two other venues turned out to be just right for the vice-presidential debate, and for the final presidential encounter, respectively: The Alley Theater in Houston and Phi Beta Kappa Hall on the campus of The College of William and Mary in Williamsburg, Virginia.

Our entire campaign staff, led by Hamilton Jordan, went into preparation mode. Briefing materials were overseen and provided by Carter's principal policy advisor, Stuart Eizenstat, with input from many sources. Once the "briefing books" had been prepared, candidate Carter took them for exhaustive study. Several days were set aside from normal campaign events prior to each of the three debates, giving our candidate plenty of time to review the great issues of the day.

Staff members, led by Jody Powell, turned to logistics. In addition to Powell, Carter's other two debate negotiators were Advertising Advisor Gerald Rafshoon and me as Television Advisor. As we met a team from the Ford campaign, a principal issue for us was to ensure that the two debaters would appear on stage equally: no presidential seal for Ford, no television coverage showing a six-foot-tall candidate looming over Carter, at five-foot-nine, and no questioners who might show favoritism. This was worked out in a series of pre-debate encounters by representatives of the two candidates.

One other task befell me, which was doling out seating tickets to our top campaign staff and supporters. This led to numerous requests to which I had to respond carefully, as each candidate had a limited number. A few days before the first debate, I was approached by Robert Strauss, the legendary Washington power broker, who had now become instrumental in the Carter campaign.

"Jagoda," he said, "I need two good tickets for the debate." Strauss, seeing me hesitate for just a few seconds as I mentally counted up where the coveted seats would go, immediately told me, "If you can't get what I need, I'll go to Governor Carter who I'm sure will help." Of course, Strauss fairly quickly got results from me. His parting remark has remained in my memory all these years later: "This will teach you to always take care of your own tickets!"

Later, Bob Strauss served in an important post as Carter's special representative for trade negotiations and, subsequently, as ambassador to the Soviet Union under President Bush. Then a widower after sixty years of marriage, Strauss retired to the Del Mar, California condo where he had spent all those years loving the Del Mar racetrack. In her fine and greatly admiring 2011 biography, *The Whole Damn Deal*, the author, Strauss' great-niece, Kathryn

McGarr, wrote that these last years would find the ambassador at his oceanside apartment window enjoying the girls' beach volleyball contests just below.

The first debate was held on September 23, at the Walnut Street Theater in Philadelphia and was moderated by the distinguished NBC News broadcaster Edwin Newman. Some may remember the twenty-seven-minute delay when the audio on the network (pool) broadcast went silent because of a technical glitch. Thankfully, just as Jerry Rafshoon got ready to go on stage to brief Carter, the sound came back.

The second debate, moderated in San Francisco's Palace of Fine Arts Theater on October 6, by NBC's Pauline Frederick—who was television news' first female star reporter—was to be remembered for President Ford's gaffe. Answering a question from Max Frankel of *The New York Times*, Ford asserted, "There is no Soviet domination of Eastern Europe." Responding vigorously, Carter said, "I would like to see Mr. Ford convince Polish-Americans and Czech-Americans and Hungarian-Americans that those countries do not live under the domination and supervision of the Soviet Union, behind the Iron Curtain."

Governor Carter and President Ford at Second Presidential Debate, Oct 6. 1976

Credit: Carter Library

Ford's comment and Carter's rebuke overwhelmed anything else from the second debate, and gave almost all fair observers the opportunity to say that Ford was the loser in the encounter. More than seventy million viewers had tuned in and, a few days later, President Ford said he had made a mistake in his characterization of the Soviets and Eastern Europe.

Then, just over a week later, on October 15, Senator Walter Mondale faced off against Senator Robert Dole in the first-ever vice presidential debate, which was held on the stage of Houston's Alley Theater. An estimated 45 million TV viewers tuned in. Post-debate polls indicated the contest was seen through partisan eyes, with both sides claiming victory. Dole had been known to be a hatchet man, and Mondale had a reputation as a strong-minded, ethical, even-handed political figure. We in the Carter/Mondale campaign camp were certain that Senator Mondale had advanced chances for our ticket.

Barbara Walters moderated the final Presidential Debate, October 22 at the College of William and Mary. The questioners were syndicated columnist Joseph Kraft, *Washington Post* editorial writer Robert Maynard, and Jack Nelson, Washington Bureau Chief of *The Los Angeles Times*. Televised in 113 nations around the globe, this debate was seen by another estimated seventy million Americans.

**Barry Jagoda as Senator Walter Mondale prepares for
1976 Vice-Presidential Debate**

Credit: Collection of Barry Jagoda

With Election Day on November 2, and only eleven days away, the race had tightened. President Ford closed the debate by asking the electorate to say, "Jerry Ford, you've done a good job, keep on doing it."

Governor Carter, in his closing remarks said, "Mr. Ford is a good and decent man, but he's been in office now more than 800 days, almost as long as John Kennedy was in office. I'd like to ask the American people what's been accomplished? A lot remains to be done."

The rest, as it is said, belongs to history. Carter won the popular vote just by two points, but garnered 297 electoral votes to Ford's 240.

Carters and Mondales in 1976 victory celebration
Credit: Carter Library

CHAPTER 3

THE WHITE HOUSE

Skillful use of legacy media—before cable news partisanship and the phenomenal rise of digital social media—became characteristic of Carter's first two years in office. This was possible because any president using the White House megaphone will always get news coverage. In those days there were no charges of "fake news." All of us in the Carter Administration knew that attacking the media and its coverage would be seen as a direct assault on First Amendment freedoms and responsibilities.

Looking back, I remember my first big assignment in the new administration was as spokesperson in Washington for President-elect Carter. We immediately established what turned out to be a huge presence, under the leadership of Transition Director Jack Watson.

We had taken over several floors of what had been the Department of Health and Welfare building, and each day dozens of reporters would stream in and out. I gave daily briefings but made virtually no news—the real action was down in the tiny village of Plains, Georgia, Carter's hometown. There the president-elect was secluded, planning strategy, and interviewing candidates for cabinet positions and other significant jobs.

When there was something important to announce, Jody Powell, the president-elect's press secretary and intimate advisor, would contact key members of the Presidential Press Corps. They had mostly left their base at the White House and started congregating as close as they could to Carter in Georgia. A temporary briefing room was established at the nearest accommodations—a motel eleven miles from Plains, in the larger town of Americus.

The real activity in Georgia was mostly unknown to hundreds of job seekers and to the many reporters still assigned to our transition headquarters, or to those who sought information from me. Politicians showed up, wanting help getting jobs in the new administration for their friends and relatives. In one memorable case, a leading Democratic senator came to see me with his very attractive, forthcoming wife who very much wanted a job in the new government.

These kinds of press and public supplications were not unusual. The process went on for three months, wearing me out, even in the thrill of it all. Of course, I was pleasant and polite to all these people. Eventually I was able to refer the job applicants to my campaign colleagues who would manage a key White House office— Presidential Personnel. This important post would initially be run by one of the campaign's favorite staff members, Jim King.

Also in that office was Jim Gammill, a brilliant young aide who eventually would be named as director of presidential personnel. During the transition and beyond, these very competent people assisted Hamilton Jordan, Carter's top aide, and the rest of us as we sorted out all the folks who wanted jobs.

Gammill had met Carter when the campaigning candidate had stayed overnight in a student suite of rooms at Harvard University. Jim was just twenty-three at the time he took on the personnel role, but charming and knowledgeable. A joke at the time was that the perfect assignment for President-elect Carter would be to head up the Army Corps of Engineers, a job that would employ many of his skills.

Of the hundreds of news media visitors wanting attention, one was particularly memorable. Pierre Salinger, President Kennedy's former press secretary, then on assignment for a French newspaper, was an old acquaintance of mine. We had met at Rice University back in 1962. Pierre needed access to some of the transition leaders to try to give his readers an idea of what to expect from the incoming administration.

I reminded Salinger of our first encounter when we had met back at Rice when I was nineteen and begged for a Kennedy White House internship he had failed to deliver. Salinger, smiling, then said something like, "Oh yeah, I remember you as a kid, and I was expecting you to come up and be an intern in the White House." It was my turn now, at age thirty-two, to consider requests from the great Mr. Salinger.

What subsequently followed over the next two years was staff work: managing the president's worldwide travels; helping him fulfill his promises to stay in close touch with the American people; selecting new leaders for the National Endowment for the Humanities: working hard to bolster National Public Radio and Public Television Broadcasting; and guiding coverage—when it could be influenced—of the then three national television networks and other major media; along with many other daily duties.

The events of the previous twelve months were almost impossible to comprehend on January 20, 1977 as I stood on the front lawn of the White House. There, President and Mrs. Carter, helped by Vice President and Mrs. Walter Mondale, reviewed the Inaugural Parade. For me, there was then no time for reflection. With me was my close campaign partner, the practical and efficient Rex Granum, soon to be Carter's deputy press secretary. After a moment Rex said, "OK, let's go!" We had a government to get underway and work was to begin immediately.

Walking over to my new suite of offices next to the White House, I found an amazing historical note in the top desk drawer. "It was from this desk that I wrote President Nixon's resignation speech," were the words penned on White House stationery and signed, *Raymond K. Price.*

Price had been a well-known top White House official. Instinctively, I knew that this little message would find a place in the Carter Presidential Library, along with hundreds of letters and official memos (copies of which I had handwritten), or original material that had come to my attention.

Of course, it was Nixon who had provided the juicy target for Carter's run for the presidency. "I will never lie to you; the American people deserve a president as good and decent as they are," Carter had promised. And now it was time for us to deliver.

My fellow staffers in the policy section had drawn up a list of several hundred promises, with input from my office. We had much to get done. I was fortunate to have as my deputy Richard M. Neustadt, a Harvard Law School-trained attorney who had worked on the campaign and had become a specialist in communications policy. Rick would become liaison with the domestic policy advisor, the amazingly competent Stuart Eizenstat. Along with Stu's deputy, a hard-working lawyer named David Rubenstein, we were deeply involved in policy planning.

Years later, Rubenstein would become a billionaire through brilliant equity fund management. I've always agreed with the view that Jimmy Carter is our best *post-president,* but Rubenstein's post-presidency career, was, itself, not too shabby. This young presidential aide was to contribute many millions of dollars for numerous projects including the restoration of the Washington Monument. Rubenstein was eventually chairman of the Kennedy Center for the Performing Arts, chairman of the Smithsonian Institution and chairman of the Council on Foreign Relations.

Besides Rick Neustadt, there was a staff of five in my spacious offices housing the special assistant to the president for media and public affairs. It included the media-savvy Anne Edwards, who would directly manage and help radio and television crews for the next four years, as they clamored for best coverage of the president. Handling our front door was Gisele Rountzounis, our secretarial assistant who had an uncanny sense of priorities.

On that first day, Rick and I hosted his father for breakfast in the staff dining room, affectionately called the *White House Mess*. The elder Richard Neustadt was a Harvard and Columbia University political scientist widely recognized as America's leading student of the presidency.

"Professor, what is the secret to presidential power?" I asked. Without hesitation, the great scholar replied, "Keep your options open!" This aphorism would be planted on my brain as we moved quickly forward. What a presidency we would have!

As President Carter's special assistant, I had been one of fourteen aides formally named by the president and announced in the press briefing room. I had become a power player in the new government, with many responsibilities—but my first tasks were to come up with and to implement new ideas for media coverage and for some sort of "direct access."

Following the lead of President Franklin Delano Roosevelt, and using his own instincts, Carter had promised to "stay in close touch with the American people." He wanted to do so beginning immediately with a direct address to the nation which was to be called a *Fireside Chat*. This term was coined not by FDR, but by Harry Butcher of the CBS Radio Network, and first used in 1933. Our first such chat would be on February 2, 1977.

Several of us had gathered in the White House residence, before a roaring fireplace. Going over plans for the event, Carter wanted to stress informality, as he would be coming directly into the living rooms of Americans. He would discuss the importance of energy conservation, and preservation of the nation's natural resources. As we were thinking about and discussing details, including what the president was to wear, Mrs. Carter said, "Why don't you wear that nice sweater Chip [his son, James Earl Carter III] got you for Christmas?" We all agreed.

President Carter's March 20, 1977 Fireside Chat

Credit: Library of Congress

Later, there was a lot of bickering over the choice of a sweater over a suit, which some argued was more presidential. Questions about the president's attire came particularly from journalists covering the White House, and White House insiders. All this led to me being cartooned by Gary Trudeau's *Doonesbury* as Secretary of Symbolism.

Portrays Barry Jagoda as Secretary of Symbolism

Credit: Garry Trudeau

No matter—Carter as president with his bully pulpit was good copy for print reporters and great television.

All presidents would like their opinions or messages delivered unfiltered, not interpreted by the press. To that end, President Carter had directed me to contact CBS News to see if they would participate in a radio call-in program, which would be a way to stay in touch with the electorate and, probably more important, give him an unfettered chance to explain some of his policies and plans. This event, which took place on March 6, 1977, was a huge success. Nine million people called the toll-free number set up by CBS News. Walter Cronkite was the moderator. As it turned out, President Carter took calls from only forty-two participants.

Here is how it started off:

CRONKITE: "Good day. President Carter and I are in the so-called Oval Office of the While House. We're in a couple of wing-back chairs in front of a coffee table. And in front of the fireplace across from us is the desk at which the President spends much of his day working; over to the left are the large doors opening out onto the beautiful Rose Garden of the White House on a very nice spring-like day here in Washington.

Cronkite and Carter, CBS News, "Ask President Carter"
Credit: Bettmann

"This is a unique occasion, and in the sense that it marks a new approach to communication between the president and the people of the United States it is indeed historic. Unique, historic, and we must also say an experiment, since a president has never taken part before in this sort of a broadcast.

"Now here's the way we want it to work, we hope it works. We'll receive phone calls from all over the country. We expect people to ask questions on many, many subjects, of course. There'll be no censorship at all, no prescreening in that sense. However, you should know that it's not going to be easy, of course, to get through to him because there have to be just a limited number of lines coming to us here at the White House.

"Now, my advice is that if you get a busy signal, you do like you do when you get a busy signal any time—you just hang up and try again. Now, when you do get through, we'll verify your call by name and hometown. And then I'll introduce you to the President and you may talk directly with him.

"Please remember that we want to give just as many of you callers as possible an opportunity to ask President Carter your questions; therefore, I'm going to be just a little bit ruthless here in cutting off any long-winded statements from our callers. We do want to hear from you, the president wants your opinions and so forth, but don't make a speech, will you? In other words, get to your question right away, ask it just as clearly and directly as possible. And, just as in presidential news conferences, you will have an opportunity for a follow-up question if you think that it's necessary.

"Mr. President, we're very pleased that you've accepted our CBS News invitation and are giving this time to let the nation *Ask President Carter.*"

PRESIDENT CARTER: "Thank you, Walter. I'm glad to have a chance to let people have direct access to me. And in the process of answering fifty to one hundred questions this afternoon—in an unrehearsed way, not knowing what's going to come next—I think the people will learn something, and I know I'll learn a lot about what is of interest to them.

"Also, I believe that if there are tens of thousands of folks who want to get through and can't do it, in listening to the other questions that are asked they're very likely to get an answer to their question.

So, I'm looking forward to the two hours and whenever you're ready, I am."

CRONKITE: "All right, Mr. President, we're ready here and I think that Joseph Willman of Sterling Heights, Michigan, is ready out there in Sterling Heights with the first question."

WILLMAN: "First of all, I'd like to say good afternoon to President Carter and Mr. Cronkite. Now, my question right now is, according to the UPI story in today's *Detroit News*, Idi Amin has said that now he has killed 7,000 Christians. With this and other happenings there, how can we with good conscience trust a man with such an ego, and if the time arises will we use force to get them out, even though a confrontation with this country is expected by Amin?"

PRESIDENT CARTER: "Well, it's hard to know how to answer that question about future events. As you know, we had what was on the border of a crisis last weekend. The attitude that we took was constantly to monitor what is going on in Uganda, to deal directly with Amin in a very forceful way to let him know that we were expecting American lives to be protected.

"We also got the help of several national leaders who are quite close to Amin, primarily those of the Moslem faith, and they contacted him directly. We also got the Federal Republic of Germany, West Germany, who has diplomatic leaders in Uganda—Entebbe, Uganda—to contact Amin. And he was constantly giving me assurance through cables that the Americans would not be hurt.

"As you know, the outcome of that weekend's tension was that he eventually said that the meeting with the Americans was called off and that anyone who wanted to leave or come into Uganda from out of the country would be permitted to do so.

"I think that it's obvious that we'll do whatever we can to protect American lives throughout the world. We have in the past, before

I became president, informed the American people in Uganda—and I might say in several other countries around the world—that there was a potentially dangerous circumstance for them. And that if they were primarily concerned with a peaceful life, they ought to change countries.

"We do know that most of the persons who are Americans in Uganda are missionaries, deeply committed to their own religious faith. They've had an option to leave and they've decided to stay.

"So, I think at this time I feel American lives there will be protected. We did act, I think, forcefully and effectively with Amin. We had a lot of help from other nations. And I can't say what I will do in the future except to try to handle the situation similarly to what I did last weekend."

The calls continued for almost two hours. At the end, Cronkite asked for the president's perception of the event.

PRESIDENT CARTER: "Walter, I liked it. The questions that come in from people all over the country are the kind that you would never get in a press conference—the news people would never raise the Ottawa Indian question. And I think it's very good for me to understand directly from the American people what they are concerned about and questions that have never been asked of me. But I want to thank you for being here with me this afternoon. The two hours passed very quickly, and I've enjoyed it and learned a lot from it."[1]

Those first heady years were the occasion for those of us close to the new president to pick up a variety of duties. There were, for example, cultural events to organize in the East Room of the White House.

---

1   For the record, the full transcript, as recorded by CBS News, is in Appendix A.

President Carter and Rosalynn particularly wanted to use the opportunity to bring extraordinary talent to be showcased at the White House. They both remembered the inspiration generated by this sort of performance when it was hosted by the Kennedy Administration.

As staff members, we had the opportunity and challenge of dealing with world-class artists such as the great Vladimir Horowitz. Once such an event would be agreed upon by the various artists and their managers, I would typically be assigned to make arrangements for live television.

Right, Barry Jagoda with Vladimir Horowitz preparing for White House concert

Credit: Carter Library

Another event I supervised was a bit more typical, but still pushed the envelope. We asked Carter's early mentor, Admiral Hyman J. Rickover, to come to the White House and launch a submarine based at Groton, Connecticut, using remote, push-button telecommunications technology we had set up adjacent to the Oval Office. This would provide another good story that could be covered by all the media.

Those of us on the Carter team knew how important Admiral Rickover had been in Carter's earlier life. As a young Annapolis graduate applying for America's submarine forces, Carter, like all aspirants, sat for a personal interview with Rickover, the head of this elite Navy team.

In that interview the admiral asked Carter, "Have you always done your best?" Replying, truthfully as he saw it, young Carter said, "No." Famously Rickover glared back at Carter and asked, "Why not your best?" which became the title of Carter's first book, one designed to explain his presidential bid. It had been just a couple of years earlier when I had read and studied this campaign tome.

Rickover's visit to the White House would be another heavily covered and discussed television opportunity. At the end of the event, though, Rickover, seemingly puzzled, turned to look for the President who had speedily left the ceremony. "I forgot to give Jimmy these papers," said the admiral. "Here," he said, as he thrust them to me. Of course, material such as this immediately went to the Staff Secretary Rick Hutcheson to be passed along to the president for possible nighttime reading.

By then, I had been getting media industry notices and accolades, but none of that was anything compared to the thrill and sense of responsibility of being a presidential advisor. It had been a genuine boost to my ego to read in the just-published *America In Search of Itself*, Theodore H. White's latest volume on the presidency, that I had been a "secret weapon" for Jimmy Carter's election.

Since 1960, White, a highly respected veteran journalist, had been the great chronicler of presidential politics. Now, in this seminal volume on the 1976 election, I was delighted that he explained how understanding the process of television news coverage was essential for winning the White House, and he wrote, "Barry Jagoda brought that dimension to the Carter campaign."

CHAPTER 4

TRIUMPHS, BUT A PHILOSOPHICAL DIFFERNCE

G ood reviews of my effectiveness were most welcome, of course, but the real satisfaction was the realization that I was helping President Carter govern a huge and often unruly country. One of our earliest challenges was trying to get rid of much of what had been called "Hollywood on the Potomac."

Carter had promised to rid the federal government of unnecessary bureaucracy and programs. With the help of a former network TV producer, Bob Lissit, we went about inventorying, across the government, the vast production and expenditure for movies and promotional films that went largely unseen. Our efforts did not necessarily please the hundreds of PR filmmakers throughout the huge federal apparatus, but many of their products were examples of the kinds of waste and inefficiency upon which Carter was waging war. After our two-year campaign, Lissit and I had shaved many hundreds of thousands of dollars in spending, with no loss of useful communication.

At the president's direction, I had also brought together a committee of leading scholars, including a now Pulitzer Prize-winning author who had been my main history advisor in college. We were to help Carter choose the head of the National Endowment for the Humanities (NEH). We worked diligently on this for a long few weeks, until finally a director was chosen. In a different process, I also helped the president select a head of National Public Radio (NPR).

Barry Jagoda reporting to President Carter in Oval Office
Credit: Carter Library

I was also the government contact, and point of approval, for the Advertising Council's program of public service announcements in radio, television and all media. Through this work, we could see that some government-related media announcements and programs had significant public value. These included public service announcements (PSAs) from the Advertising Council, which ranged from promotions by Smokey Bear ("Only you can prevent forest fires"), to warnings about cigarettes and health.

I heard, by memo from the President, and during an Oval Office meeting, that he approved of my work with the Ad Council, and with the monitoring of duplication and waste in Federal media outreach programs. Carter loved these efforts, especially when valuable public work could be done by the private sector with limited help from government, and at no cost to the taxpayer.

One of my most important assignments was to stay in regular touch with the Washington bureau chiefs of NBC, CBS, and ABC. From my journalism career, I already knew each of these gatekeepers very well, on a first-name basis. We would need their cooperation when requesting national television time for an important speech, or even for such obviously newsworthy events as a televised news conference. These executives had to be assured that news would be forthcoming if their organizations were to air live programs from the White House. So, before we even scheduled a Carter news conference, we made sure the timing would not unduly pre-empt regularly scheduled programs, including those in prime time.

First established as regular live events by President Eisenhower, these news conferences were excellent ways to reach the American public. Carter, with his lightning-fast mind, was particularly effective in these situations. Still, we always prepared briefing books and there was almost never a policy or political gaffe by Carter in these live television events.

Although most of our efforts focused on domestic policy and bolstering the US economy, President Carter immediately stepped onto the world stage. One of the President's first initiatives was his plan to relinquish the Panama Canal. On September 7, 1977, Carter signed an agreement revoking the seventy-five-year-old treaty, which had granted to the United States permanent control of the Panama Canal. This old arrangement had resulted in growing protests in Panama and throughout South America. Under the terms of Carter's new treaty, the United States maintained the right to defend the canal up until the year 2000, when Panama would regain full autonomy,

So, the Latin American advisor to the president, Robert Pastor, and I were assigned to the first of several trips to Panama to make final arrangements.

On our first night in Panama City, we stumbled onto one of the untold "perks of office," another amazing experience of those White House years. Panamanian President Omar Trujillo was welcoming, offering us a great meal and instructing his then-Intelligence Chief Manuel Noriega to "give these boys the kind of welcome to Panama they deserve." We watched as two beyond-beautiful women, perhaps in their twenties, came to us, apparently intended to be our girlfriends during our stay. Married to a daughter of former Secretary of Defense Robert McNamara, Pastor looked the other way. As a young divorced, somewhat wild guy, I immediately fell in love, but had to restrain myself.

We were on official White House business and had much serious work to undertake. There were the final agreement papers, which Pastor consented to on behalf of President Carter. Then we were whisked away in a Panamanian military helicopter to the site where the formal agreement would be signed. There I took a good look around to be able to give recommendations to the political and scheduling staffs about how the return ceremony should be arranged.

Back in Washington, these preparations were set aside as we now were tasked with convincing the American people that the return of the Panama Canal was not traitorous. There was strong opposition in the Senate, but Carter ultimately prevailed by a small majority.

But the president's problems were ongoing, as he went about searching for political change on a treacherous world stage.

American alliances around the world were more or less normal when President Carter began his historic global journey at the end of 1977. His first stop was in Warsaw, but at the airport, a series of gaffes by the State Department-supplied translator led to embarrassing press coverage. Along with misinterpreting Carter's hope to learn about the Polish people's desires for the future as, "I desire the Poles carnally," *The Washington Post* reported that the translator also misinterpreted the president's praise for the Polish Constitution of 1791 as, instead, ridicule. Carter described when he left the United States and it was translated as, "When I abandoned the United States." When Carter said, "Poland is the ancestral home of more than six million Americans, *The New York Times* reported that it came out as, "a state also which constitutes the fatherland of ten million Americans."

The next stop was Iran, a vital ally during the Cold War, with American fighter planes on the tarmac in Teheran aimed at the Soviet Union. That decades-long conflict was coming to an end, and the Shah of Iran would soon no longer be under US protection. But it was New Year's Eve, and the Shah and his spouse, the Shabanu, regaled the president and his traveling party with a never-to-be-forgotten celebration. Our eyes bulged as we witnessed the spread of food, music and dancing to welcome in 1978. This turned out to be one of the last grand occasions of the Shah's regime.

We arose with difficulty the next morning, New Year's Day, to continue our eleven-nation state visit travels, but none of our group would dare sleep in as President Carter was ready to get going, heading for New Delhi, India, where he was to address the Indian parliament.

At that point in time, none of us could have then imagined that the subsequent fall of the Shah would end with a bloodless coup, the installation of a religious zealot, and the taking of more than sixty American hostages.

Carter subsequently ordered a secret effort using helicopters and commandos to free the hostages, but the mission failed, crashing into the desert. The fiasco damaged Carter's re-election bid.

Ronald Reagan was elected, and as a snub, the Americans were released on Carter's last day in office. The Iranian dilemma—an overwhelming foreign policy problem—has persisted until the present day.

Much more success came because President Carter had long had his sights on peace efforts between Israel and the Arabs. To the amazement of the world, there eventually emerged a first-step agreement, the one at Camp David that resulted after hard negotiations between Israel's Menachem Begin and the Egyptian leader, Anwar Sadat. President Carter had personally spent ten wrenching days forging a historic deal between these passionate leaders.

Camp David Agreement, Sadat, Carter, Begin, September 17, 1978
Credit: National Archives

Even with the Camp David triumph, Carter's struggles continued. It was not only Iran and the hostage crisis fiasco. At home, oil prices—with long lines at gasoline pumps—and economic inflation, which reached twenty-one percent before the end of his term, were causing turmoil. Many advisors began to be nervous about his re-election prospects.

Some pressed for acceptance of "the permanent campaign," an approach I had deeply opposed. Their idea would be to manage Carter's message, and for him to stick to talking points that reflected well on his performance or in popular initiatives.

Sidney Blumenthal, a reporter, who had written a book with that same title, had first evoked the phrase in print.

In fact, that volume, *The Permanent Campaign*, devoted numerous pages to my own efforts to help support President Carter's private promise not to use his newly elected post just to get re-elected.

I was deeply involved in President Carter's vow to be open with the American people, putting policy considerations ahead of politics. But, as two years had elapsed, now into 1978, other advisors embraced permanent-campaign strategies, finally convincing the president to change tactics. That meant, in part, not being as fully candid with the American people. Carter instead would be "on message."

My strongly held view was that Carter should continue to be open and transparent, that his brilliant mind was most effectively on display when he was seemingly extemporaneous and improvisational.

As Blumenthal wrote, "Barry Jagoda, with wide experience in broadcast journalism worked in the campaign and in the White House. He wanted Carter to be spontaneous."

I knew that to the extent that television cameras have the function of bringing people where they couldn't otherwise go, it's important not to be contrived. The truth has a way of surfacing, I warned. Within the White House I was saying that the key to Carter was vulnerability. I said he had to take chances.

My perspective made an opponent of someone far more influential than the campaign's pollster, Patrick Caddell, or advertising man Gerald Rafshoon. When Rosalynn Carter decided that my approach might be threatening to her husband, of course my options narrowed considerably.

At the time, I told author Blumenthal that "I should have talked to Rosalynn long ago," and he quoted me on that in his book. She was very open-minded, but her political fears, concerns and pressures had taken over.

Inside the White House, I knew that the very savvy Mrs. Carter had taken on a role of that of the "ordinary American." From the moment I stepped into the Carter home in Plains, early in 1976, I immediately realized that her opinion was considered by her husband to be a bellwether.

Rosalynn and I had gotten along especially well. On that day in January 1976, she and Carter asked me to accompany her to a nearby village charity softball game. She was fun and charming and almost as determined as her husband. They had already gone through decades of political success, and some failure. But, of course, as with so many spouses, when her husband followed her thinking, he could do no wrong.

But now, going into three years of his presidency, Rosalynn was perturbed that her Jimmy was not being perceived as a man of great accomplishment. Maybe he seemed to be too spontaneous, unstructured and uncontrolled. She also began to think that the White House ought to settle on a few themes easily accessible to the average American.

Blumenthal quoted me, "After I spouted off about the need for vulnerability, it drove Rosalynn off the wall." Further, he wrote, "She wondered if Jagoda was trying to expose Jimmy?" Meantime, Blumenthal added, "Rafshoon was saying to Rosalynn, 'We should let Jimmy project two or three themes.'"

I didn't think a president with a mind like Carter's could have just two or three themes. The world is more complicated, I argued vociferously and passionately to Jerry Rafshoon and Rosalynn.

But, meanwhile, unbeknownst to me, Rosalynn acted. She talked with Jerry. They agreed that Carter needed a consistent image. Rafshoon decided that his new task would be to narrow the presidency down to a few themes.

Barry Jagoda with President Carter in Oval Office

Credit: White House photograph

Eventually, I went to the Oval Office to talk to Carter about it. I knew that the president couldn't have two media advisers. He was warm, he wished me good luck, wanted me to stay around in some other role, but said there was "a philosophical difference" about the way forward. I offered my resignation as his special assistant, which he accepted on most generous terms.

I would enthusiastically move on to a new assignment in the White House, which turned out to be another extraordinary experience. I became part of the Carter foreign policy decision-making apparatus at Zbigniew Brzezinski's National Security Council (NSC).

CHAPTER 5

DIPLOMACY
AND LEGACY

I well remember Carter's admonition at our first senior staff meeting, on day one of the Administration: "We will begin by making sure everyone in this room knows how to spell Zbig's name: Brzezinski, that is B-R-Z-E-Z-I-N-S-K-I, repeat after me!" And damn if he didn't spell it again, an insistent teacher for a staff that was obviously willing to learn.

My new media-focused responsibility was as general assistant working the next seven months for National Securtiy Adviser Brzezinski. This was invaluable experience. I was now cheek by jowl with Madeline Albright, who was then the official spokesperson for the NSC and later, of course, Secretary of State in the Clinton Administration. We had a relatively small staff that included such eventual luminaries as the future Secretary of Defense Robert Gates, the nation's leading authority on Iranian politics and well-published Professor Gary Sick and, my friend, that highly knowledgeable and very flexible Latin American specialist, Bob Pastor.

There were more than a dozen other important players, including the soon-to-be famous Richard Holbrooke, who along with Secretary of State Warren Christopher, was to negotiate the Dayton Agreement for peace in Bosnia and Herzegovina. Among my lasting colleagues from those days is Robert Hunter, an incisive policy analyst focusing on Western Europe. A very dear friend from UT days, Allen "Tex" Harris, had risen to top leadership positions in the American Foreign Service Association, the grouping of more than 15,000 professional diplomats. Quietly, I consulted with the NSC staff on how best to get their perspectives into the flow of news.

The NSC was coordinated for Zbig by his deputy David Aaron, a solid policy analyst, with a good sense of the politically possible. For me this was truly a graduate education in foreign policy management.

During this time, I frequently thought back to the admonition of my University of Texas international relations professor, the incisive James Roach. He taught that the goal of American foreign policy—of any nation's international policy, he argued—was to work in a way so that other countries did not disagree with the home country's goals.

One of Roach's best students, from over many decades teaching thousands at UT, was my classmate and close buddy, Richard L. Cohen, who was eventually to be staff director for the world-class pollster and analyst Dan Yankelovich. Together, as best colleagues, Richard and I have now traversed the shoals of personal and public life over the past sixty years.

Richard had been a Rhodes Scholar and a star international exchange student, one of hundreds of my classmates at UT who traveled on such programs to Chile and elsewhere over many years. Most thereby gained first-hand understandings of life and governing around the world.

In 1977, Cohen had agreed to serve in the Carter government as a top foreign policy aide to the then-director of the United States Information Agency and extraordinary scholar, Ambassador John Reinhardt. Together with agency deputy Charles Bray, they directed the soft diplomacy work of nearly 7,000 employees whose jobs ranged from managing and producing *The Voice of America* to supervising international exchange programs, and to serving as the spokespersons in each of the more than 150 American embassies around the world.

I had heard numerous times, from Ambassador Reinhardt himself, of how valuable Richard Cohen was in the functioning of this vast and important agency. It was an honor to be there when Richard was sworn in for a job in which he would perform brilliantly—as he did throughout his life as well.

Left, Ambassador John Reinhardt Director USIA, as Richard L. Cohen, right, named top aide, with Barry Jagoda, center

Credit: United States Information Agency

After his Carter Administration service, Cohen was a founder of Institutional Shareholder Services (ISS) that became the world's leading provider of corporate governance, monitoring responsible investing by boards of directors. Richard's wife, the wonderfully talented Grisselle, had been a highly respected teacher of French and of Spanish and eventually became a top Washington, DC stockbroker. They continue to be treasured life-long friends.

As I served the president, my life had intersected with so many brilliant people.

My exit from the White House was fortuitous, because it would have been difficult to watch the eventual implosion close up. But 1980, unfortunately, was too soon upon Carter, when the optimistic Californian Ronald Reagan was to deliver a few painful lessons. What had happened to the Carter presidency and its amazingly erudite leader was best summed up by one of the President's former chief speechwriters, Jim Fallows. He later wrote, "Carter had fifty solutions to problems, but Reagan had only one slogan." This may well have provided an explanation for why Carter was moved out after Reagan was elected in 1980.

For me, all the many journeys with President Carter are remembered mostly with great pleasure. I gained a sense of successfully moving beyond journalism, and becoming focused as what I now think of as a more fully rounded citizen of the nation.

These adventures gave us, in his entourage, more than one chance to ask and try to answer the continuing question: Who was, or is, Jimmy Carter? The first explanation that I have is, perhaps, the most obvious. He was really smart. It was also apparent that this was a pious man. We knew about his religiosity from the start, and we knew that this would always be his way. Even as a candidate, he would brag that he read the Holy Scriptures each day in Spanish. And of course, Carter was a very determined patriot.

Years later, and at this writing the oldest living former President, Carter still taught Sunday school in a church near the tiny Georgia town of Plains. On a visit there in 2018, I could still catch elements of the essential Carter. One of his sermons reminded the congregation that there was no value in avoiding difficult tasks because of stumbling blocks put in your way by others.

On that occasion at church, as was their habit, Jimmy and Rosalynn (his wife then of more than seventy years) responded to questions from many of the visitors who had stood in line to hear them. One question, and their answers, I clearly remember: "What would you recommend to young persons now trying to figure out a major occupation in life?" Almost in tandem, the Carters responded, "Public health—that is where one can find satisfaction." That made sense because, thanks to The Carter Center they had established, there were now ongoing worldwide programs of wellness and life improvement for the world's most needy.

As I have suggested, Jimmy Carter's many years of post-presidential life and accomplishments have been much commented upon and became the subject of a book by one of America's pre-eminent historians, Rice University Professor Douglas Brinkley. In that volume, Brinkley details the hundreds of small and dozens of large qualities that Carter has exhibited since he was removed from office by the brilliant efforts of Ronald Reagan. Of course, as we have seen, the Iranian hostage-taking, twenty-one percent inflation and a promise by Reagan to bring back "morning to America" had their impact.

My explanation for Carter's post-presidential success is that, with the help of a few trusted aides, Carter finally shed the burdens of managing hundreds of thousands of federal and military workers, and the challenge of dealing with a very hostile external world. As a former president, he has shown his own true character and mighty intelligence, now freed from the mistakes of others. Now truly his own man, Jimmy Carter became the person he promised he would be: "As good and decent as the American people themselves."

When I left the White House, I had considered writing a book about my experiences there. I even wrote a proposal, but dropped the idea because my feelings about Carter were conflicted. I had seen his wonderful leadership qualities up close, but I also knew the president could be rather impatient, which led him to be cutting, even nasty, to some who were working for him. For instance, once he gave an assignment to a trustworthy and hard-working staff member who worked diligently to respond. But when the results were eventually presented, Carter's response, from behind those steely blue eyes, was, "Thanks, but if that is the best you can do, I could have handled the assignment myself."

My conflict about the man and those around him stemmed from my belief—and professional experience—that in public life you can't buy control of journalism. You're not selling a product. You can't control news coverage, and a political leader must expect to be open to scrutiny. You can't manage the message just by managing what the president says—or does not say. That was my strong view then, and

I think at least some of that notion has stood the test of time now that our nation is deeply embroiled in looking toward the election of 2020. Politicians are packaged and presented as products, but with even more intense media coverage, they cannot manage the message.

A significant change in the media landscape, since the years before the election of 1980, is the appearance of at least three *point-of-view* cable television networks. And using any one of hundreds of social media outlets, almost anyone can assume the title of *journalist.* The consumer's challenge, then, is to spot which communications channels are being managed with integrity. The current endless media options also provide politicians with media channels—be it online, Twitter, Facebook or biased cable media channels—with advocates who will manipulate headlines to favor their candidates. Fox News makes no apologies for spinning news to benefit conservatives and Donald Trump, while MSNBC is largely seen as a voice for Democrats and liberals.

Is it any surprise that the country and its voting electorate has become so polarized? In the bad old days, there was an idle dream among politicians that they might order up a newspaper or other news outlet to carry only the news one wanted. Unfortunately, that wish has now nearly come true.

I argue in this book that a political leader must know how to weave in and around news outlets that fit these polarized perspectives. Case in point is the incumbent, Donald Trump, who has upwards of sixty million followers on one or the other of these forms of public communication, where he regularly uses his personal Twitter account for government business.

President Trump is the perfect bully for the "bully pulpit" that is the White House. Trump has become his own media advisor, working through his very intelligent son-in-law, the Harvard College and Harvard Law School graduate Jared Kushner. In turn, Kushner directs the spending of huge sums of money by the official Trump campaign chairperson Brad Parscale, a consultant and political aide who served as the digital media director for Trump's very successful 2016 presidential campaign. This dangerous operative, whose integrity flows completely with the whims and values of President Trump, now serves as the campaign manager for the president's 2020 reelection efforts.

A central theme of this volume, my own adventures in traditional and new media, requires much further reflection when I am confronted by Trump and his huge base of American voters. Perhaps unfairly, the former secretary of state and 2016 Democratic standard bearer, Hillary Clinton, called this segment of the electorate "deplorables." Mrs. Clinton may have been justified in her naming, but such campaign rhetoric did not help in the election contest with Trump. Though Clinton received nearly three million more votes in the popular count, her losses in key Electoral College states now seem, in part, to be the result of her occasional bad presentations, as much as that of the lucky and brilliant campaign run by Trump, often as a demagogue.

Television and media advisors for the 2020 Democratic nominee, trying to unseat the incumbent, will have to be extremely careful. The current occupant of the Oval Office is a vicious name-caller, frequently given to spouting lies. According to reliable counts from CNN and *The Washington Post*, in his first thousand days as president, Trump said nearly 14,000 things that were either misleading or outright false. One smart media advisor I know refuses to use the proper designation of *Mr. President,* instead calling him *Mr. Tweet*—a kind nickname, indeed. I can only contrast the heinous behavior of the current president with the imperfect but noble public servant who I served for three years.

I look back to those brighter times, toiling from dawn to dusk at Jimmy Carter's side. Without expressing gratuitous thinking, I can say those were times mostly characterized by integrity from the president and his closest staff members. The Carter presidency may be silhouetted as a time of genuine work to benefit the American people, while the Trump presidency presents a threat to our nation, our Constitution, and the moral fiber of all Americans.

PART II

GROWING UP

CHAPTER 6

ROOTS AND RISINGS

T ypical of early twentieth century immigrants, my family members figured out how to survive—and then some. There were two branches—the Fradins in New York City tenements, and the Jagodas—both soon to unite in the precincts of industrial Ohio.

For her part, my mom, a Fradin, had been brought to this country before World War I, as one of four siblings from Kiev, Ukraine. None of them had learned the tongue of their new country before they arrived. Mother, though, was a free spirit. She was early to get a driver's license and was a commuter from the steel mill zones of Youngstown, Ohio to the metropolis of Cleveland for medical school.

Mother's open mind catapulted her from grade school to medical school in a short generation. She fell in love and married her virtually unschooled husband, whose book-learning ended in the ninth grade. But my dad had many compensating virtues, including being headstrong, courageous and everlastingly idealistic.

Saul and Anne Jagoda as newlyweds
Credit: Collection of Barry Jagoda

The reason these two kids ended up in the industrial zones of Youngstown was because their families had settled there among accepting immigrant relatives. After my paternal grandmother came to the US with her two baby sons—Uncle Harry and my dad—the learning came quickly. She was the Polish-Jewish daughter of a prosperous timber merchant/sugar factory owner. When she married my granddad, Morris Jagoda, he was counseled by his father-in-law to "get out of Poland or you will quickly be drafted into the imperial army of the lord, the Tsar of Russia."

Frightened, or now worldly-wise, my grandfather had gotten to America and ironically, within a short while after arriving, he was drafted into the United States Army where he served during World War I. Before he returned home to Ohio, he had been gassed for his troubles.

For the rest of his life, "Zeidy" was a handyman, and worked for a time in the warehouse of Youngstown's main department store. To round out our family, these grandparents had a third child, an American-born daughter to go with the two growing boys. Decades later I retrieved what has become a treasured photo: me, my elderly grandmother with her daughter, my beloved Aunt Evelyn, and my mom.

Left to right: Evelyn Solnik, Anne Jagoda, Rachel Jagoda, Barry Jagoda

Credit: Collection of Allan Solnik

As our whispered family legend had it, I was to be aborted because my mom didn't want a baby while she was in medical school. Apparently, my paternal grandmother (my "Bubbe"), who promised to look after me, saved my life. Later, along with my own exposure to the evils of necessarily back-alley abortions, as a young unmarried guy with a pregnant girlfriend, I had always wondered whether anyone should allow the choice of the mother to be denied. But what if that abortion—of me—had gone forward against my mother's will?

Even more dramatic than my dad's father being gassed, while he was a soldier in the US Army, was the sad story following my mom's mother getting her brood of three daughters and a son through the portals of Ellis Island. Thirteen months later, the mother was dead of pneumonia. The family had to survive without her, although her spouse, my maternal grandfather, Jacob Fradin, lived on.

To be sure, as it turned out, my parents benefitted from being young immigrant children as they had quickly assimilated into American life. My dad became a serial entrepreneur and my mother, though speaking no English when she arrived, quickly worked her way through twelve grades and went on to receive her medical degree.

And they did all this despite having one foot in the old-country ways that their own parents had brought with them, reflecting being part of the large Yiddish-speaking culture that immigrated to America in the early twentieth century.

The only story I remember from these early times is the one about the evil Doberman Pinscher that is said to have attacked my father when, as a neighborhood grocer, Dad delivered the product of his butcher. This was the family lore. As might be expected, to this day I cringe every time I see one of these beautiful beasts.

This era in American life would be put in intellectual perspective by the seminal works of Oscar and Mary Handlin, scholars of the America immigrant experience. In this case the Handlin work would make clearer the larger context of my family's journey to citizenship.

These stories of the roots of my family are similar to the history told in *A Good Family,* the 2019 book by Pulitzer Prize-winning historian David Maraniss. There, in an often-detached reportorial tone, the author describes the Constitutional violations imposed on his parents, who, like mine, had leftist values. Unlike mine, though, Maraniss' father was an American communist.

There are many such stories of the loss of First Amendment freedoms. Not the least of these is described in *American Prometheus,* the brilliant 2007 biography of J. Robert Oppenheimer by Kai Bird and Martin Sherwin. Prometheus was the Greek god who was believed to have brought fire to man, and like him, Oppenheimer is known as the father of the atomic bomb. The book, however, details that the bedroom of Oppenheimer's communist girlfriend (later his wife) was wiretapped by the FBI, and how the US government, instead of high praise for the Promethean Oppenheimer, merely stripped him of his security clearances. President Truman had tried to name the distinguished scientist, this upper-class graduate of Harvard, with a PhD from Cambridge, to a high-level position based on his contributions to ending World War II, but Oppenheimer ended up as another victim of the "red scare," based on his politics.

My own assimilating family made quick economic progress. My dad had established himself as a quality grocer in a fancy neighborhood of Youngstown, Ohio. But things suddenly fell apart when Daddy received doctor's orders to move out of the cold Ohio winters. We would move to Phoenix, Arizona, where they would start over. My parents—using Ohio savings—bought a motel to run, but they did not lose their steadfast ingrained idealism.

Despite my father being an entrepreneurial capitalist, my parents retained their passion for the left-wing ideology, which bordered on American communism pretty much following the Stalinist line. It would have been no surprise that among the guests at their Phoenix motel—named the Alamo Plaza in commemoration of a moment of great patriotism—were the great Paul Robeson and the less well-known but even more fervent Marxist, Gus Hall, the reigning chair of the Communist Party of the United States.

All these extreme leftists were seeking ways to express their views on racism, civil rights and related matters. For some the Communist Party was, apparently, the vehicle they chose.

Beginning in very early childhood, I was a silent observer to the falling apart of the family. Sister, an attractive teen, had her boyfriends at the new high school in Phoenix. Daddy was trying to run the motel—for which he had no background—and he somehow got Mother to become the facility's maid. With her medical degree and with more empty rooms than those rented out, she soon expressed disillusion.

Phoenix might have been good place for our family of four, which included my sister Lou Beth, ten years my senior and now a budding teenager. But this motel near-miss led to bankruptcy.

My earliest memory of the falling apart was when Mom gave up and tried to escape these circumstances, running away through the oleander bushes and ditches near the motel. Fearing abandonment, I chased after her. In a certain way, my psyche never recovered from this trauma. Fortunately, only two years went by before Daddy knew he had to try something else, especially after a new highway siphoned traffic away from the motel.

Our salvation came when a Youngstown acquaintance, someone from the Jewish community, dangled a solution—and my dad grabbed it. Almost before any of us knew what he was doing, Daddy had us moved to Houston, where money was supplied to start up a grocery store with a heavy soft drink and beer component. Our benefactor was a guy named Joe Darsky.

In olden Youngstown days, Joe's mother had started a tiny beverage operation. She mixed "sodas" into cold drinks and washed the bottles when they came back. Joe, as a creative young adult, turned this into a profitable soft drink company, and he was clever enough to expand to the Sunbelt. There, the company, called Golden Age Beverages, filled a huge demand for cold drinks in the hot and now-beginning-to-boom Houston.

So, again, my Dad was to start up his own business.

CHAPTER 7

HOMETOWN HOUSTON

Weather was again a big factor in the change of geography. Because Houston was so hot and humid, my dad established what quickly became a very successful little business. Always the idealist, Daddy called his little convenience stores *Help-Us-Totem*. The big chain in the area was then known as *U-Totem*. My father's dawn-to-midnight work there paid the mortgage for a house we soon owned in a redneck community, not far from his stores. He had opened a second beer joint just two blocks from what was then the world's largest oil refinery, later to be part of Exxon.

Saul Jagoda and "Help-Us Totem" delivery van

Credit: Collection of Barry Jagoda

To make his operations work efficiently, and for a reasonable commute, Daddy bought us a post-WWII GI bungalow in the working-class part of suburban Houston known for its proximity to the Houston Ship Channel. I was six and my sister had finished high school and gotten into the University of Houston.

The Jagodas were the only Jews for many miles in the Houston area's industrial neighborhoods. This didn't mean much to my parents since, as Marxists, they had also become atheists. A long drive to the nearest synagogue was irrelevant to them.

My mother, as mentioned, was trained in medicine (with a degree in podiatric chiropody from Cleveland's famed Case Western Reserve University), but she declined to take the state board exams in Texas: she was exhausted from cleaning rooms at the motel, and was now the full-time wife of a constantly working absent husband. This was also where part of the "red scare" in American political culture came up to bite our family. Mom, the second of the two Constitutional idealists in our family, later told me she had refused to sign the required Texas medical certification documents that merely had her say that she was loyal to the United States, which, of course, she was. This kind of stubbornness was to haunt our family forever.

Decades later, famous from my White House stint, I was a guest in the fancy Mexican vacation home of an important journalist in the resort town of San Miguel de Allende. The hostess, Elizabeth Carpenter, who also had been a top aide in the White House of Lady Bird and Lyndon Johnson, asked the twelve of us seated at the dinner table, "What formed you?" For me there could be only one answer. I was formed by the fear of being called un-American. When a child discovers, hidden at home as I had done, papers warning of what to do if called before a congressional investigating committee, called the House Un-American Activities Committee (HUAC), the scar would last a lifetime.

It was this fear of our government, along with anger at the Kennedy-Johnson Vietnam War policy, that propelled me away from the civic life of my hometown. Instead of making an otherwise obvious middle-class turn to the law as my profession, I seized upon another opportunity: the one to watch my own government. But later as I became a more mature professional, entering my fourth decade, I realized that running away from responsibility was not an answer to my fear of government.

Houston in 1950 was a city of less than 500,000. But the population began to explode just as we arrived. The explanation for the huge increase was tied to its location as an emerging petrochemical center. But everybody also knew that few would happily come to this city until air conditioning arrived: the weather in this low-lying Gulf of Mexico region was miserable.

There were, generally, two reasons for living in Houston. Both were tied to economic opportunity: the first being associated with part of a traditional family; the second, to pursue your fortune. Over the years, plenty of Houstonians had quickly gotten wealthy after moving to this energy-centered industrial city. Later generations of those families, of course, stayed to reap the benefits.

So, there we were, new Houstonians—but living in Jacinto City, a small working-class town that abutted Houston, with mainly redneck neighbors also new to the booming region. Many of the kids on my street, La Crosse, and in the nearby neighborhood, were devotees of vacation Bible school. But being from a Jewish culture, I knew better than to be drawn into this sort of evangelism.

More difficult to grasp were the leftist leanings that I later learned were part of my parents' understanding of life and politics: I eventually was taught that this was their way of manifesting commitments to civil rights and world peace.

But for me, in general, life seemed moderately tranquil with few concerns as I entered elementary school. My educational crisis would come just a few years later.

At John Greenleaf Whittier Elementary School, of course I stood out, as I was from a literate family, including parents who cared about ideas. But the first big mistake came with the decision of my teachers, the principal and my parents to have me skip part of the first grade.

So, for the rest of primary and secondary school, I was with a small cohort of kids who, for various reasons, were always in the wrong half of the grade, either because they had started school in mid-year, or they had been held back. Because I had always been promoted on merit before this, I was the exception among most of my classmates. I sensed this was a problem, but could never fully articulate the trouble.

Only sixty years later, when I was helping to promote faculty research at the University of California, did I learn that the most important indicator of student achievement was one's peer group—not class size, and not necessarily the quality of the teacher. I had landed in a mess.

The worst part of life for me as a young boy was that my father was almost always away from home, opening his store by 7 am and closing not earlier than 11 pm. This caused parental arguments around the house and left me wondering when Daddy would be home. We never sat together at the dinner table, and the cultural absences were worse. Never in my childhood was music played at home, nor did Daddy find much time for books. Mom collected *Readers Digest* distillations, and some other old books joined them on our shelves. Like many who had grown up in the Depression years, my mother was careful about spending pennies, and larger sums much more so.

When I now write about growing up on the wrong side of the tracks, of course this is a perception I picked up in later years. At the time, I suspected there was something wrong, but kids don't really know enough to question their environment. You just try to fit in. My father did find time to be president of the local Lions Club and for their annual light bulb sales. When I accompanied him to Lions Club events, I received a good bit of attention. Daddy, known in the community as Mr. Jay, was widely appreciated for his good community service, and I was praised on those public occasions with the words, "So, you are Mr. Jay's son!"

Barry as proud Cub Scout
Credit: Collection of Barry Jagoda

We did have a Cub Scout pack, and Mother drove us downtown to Houston's fanciest department store where I was fitted for my uniform.

Possibly the best quality of our household geography was our home's location, which was just a short distance from uncut woods. This wildness nearby would not challenge theories about the end of the American frontier, but the trees and the acres nearby made me feel like Davy Crockett with my very own wild frontier.

Many years later, when I would drive by to visit my childhood home, the presence of a new interstate highway running right through the old woods was shocking. Later, global warming affected the woods, and eventually, flooding even closed down parts of the new highway. Our little working-class suburb had been sacrificed to the growth of Houston, which would become America's fourth-largest city. But it was in the pre-interstate Jacinto City, a small community bordering Houston, that I spent my childhood.

My academic career at Whittier Elementary continued, and after sixth grade we all transferred to J.W. Oates, the designated junior high for kids on my side of the suburb, but still a dozen miles away. It was at Oates that my education stalled. Even now, many decades later, I'm not so sure of what had happened there or what I learned. I went from being a standout student to a life of anonymity and mediocrity.

At just under five-and-a half feet, I was no candidate for sports. And in the classroom, it began to appear that I was not going to achieve math prowess or even make a decent showing as a student of arithmetic. This math fear and my limited skill in abstract reasoning was to haunt me the rest of my life. I would be unprepared to join the computer revolution.

Fortunately, after surviving two years at Oates, it was time to get to what seemed to be a better chance: at the new McReynolds Junior High. There things got better for me. I was still undernourished intellectually, but a drama club, a typing teacher and a driver's education teacher made things seem as if I had a chance to make progress.

Later in life, I realized these early formative years were pretty much squandered. Compared to others, I was neither introduced to any canon of literature nor to any decent study of history. Most of us at McReynolds were never expected to go on to college, and although the training there in wood shop and other vocational courses had benefits, it clearly routed us away from a more college-bound direction.

My saving grace at McReynolds was a music teacher, Mr. Batista, under whose tutelage I received some elemental music training on the violin. Luckily, in another arena, Mr. Herman Lefkowitz was very helpful in spite of his role as the school's head football and basketball coach, which seemed unlikely to me. But, perhaps because he was Jewish, Coach Lefkowitz took a shine to me.

I was made manager of the McReynolds basketball squad, and this was my initiation into team sports. This was helpful because it began laying the foundation for behind-the-scenes jobs I would go on to hold as an adult with professional teams in Houston, even if the main function of my junior high assignment was to be sure that the towels were properly retrieved in the locker room and that the players had plenty of ice for their bruises, and drinking water. By then, I was in the ninth grade and my mom worked to get me a hardship driver's license at age fourteen. Texas was ridiculously lenient in some categories such as this, but this privilege meant that I could drive myself to school and home after sports practices.

Often, when I did get home to La Crosse Street, Mom would be helping at the stores. By now, Daddy had now expanded his convenience store-beer joint business to three locations. Mom would likely be at one of the sites, so it was a relief that I was on my own for commuting to school. But I was often lonely because there was no one home when I did get back after my sports managerial chores. I can't remember how I spent these late afternoons, but it was surely not with homework or books. Occasionally, I would go over and sweep up at the store or see what running a small business might entail.

Barry's parents Anne and Saul Jagoda
Credit: Collection of Barry Jagoda

One memory does stick out—a steel plant worker, after a couple of extra beers at Dad's store, made an anti-Semitic slur: "You Jew, why don't you go back to where you came from." My dad instantly reached into the ice chest, took out a beer bottle, broke it over the bar so that the jagged neck showed, and said, "You bastard, leave my premises and never come back." Daddy was always my hero for that. In retrospect, my parents were heroic to me in many ways, even beyond their normal parental responsibilities—care, feeding and providing a moral dimension.

The next step in my education was getting into Austin High School, geographically another center of low-income demographics. What I remember about that first spring semester of high school—the low tenth grade—was that almost everybody else would be at the proper tenth grade beginning in the fall. Anyway, I joined Reserve Officers' Training Corps (ROTC), the US Army's program for young students.

ROTC was no fun and almost as unpleasant to me as the alternative—physical education. In ROTC, I was introduced to the M-1 rifle, the predecessor to the M-16, which was a lighter weapon for the emerging Cold War. In a weird irony, those weapons had been knocked off from the lighter-weight Soviet Kalashnikov rifle. There, in 10th grade ROTC, I first learned the immortal basic training chant: "This is my rifle, and this is my gun. One is for fighting and one is for fun!" What was even more lasting was the black-and-blue M-1 thumb quickly acquired by this novice who had learned how to use his weapon the hard way.

I had thought the worst aspect of life in Houston was the deplorable weather. But the city provided a decent income for my family. The refinery shift workers needed cold beer at the end of their workday, and my father's convenience stores provided that.

These same petrochemical plants provided decent hourly wages for a large and growing workforce. Eventually, my family members moved on from the convenience store business and established steel and industrial supply companies that manufactured and sold materials needed to rebuild plants. These family businesses (eventually with hundreds of workers) could generate substantial profits selling new valves, pipes and steel for rebuilding. The companies purchasing the products were relatively unconcerned about large markups because they needed supplies immediately.

One thoughtful friend, whose father had become an engineering superintendent at that world's largest oil refinery, told me that he was then more worried about the plant blowing up than he was about "the Russkies." During the Cold War, most Americans had a view of Russians as bad people. Houstonians' fear of infrastructure explosions and industrial pollution was something everybody learned to live with, as a downside of good profits for the industrialists and good wages for a growing workforce.

William K. Nemzin, my beloved brother-in-law, well-educated with engineering studies, once told me—comparing natural disasters, not the man-made kind—"here at the Texas Gulf Coast we always had a few days' notice when a hurricane was coming, but you folks in California never knew when an earthquake was going to hit."

Bill was mostly right. My own fear, when I eventually lived in the midst of the idyllic climate and lifestyle of coastal California, was that my family and home would be torn to shreds by an earthquake. My other concern—this one for our whole country, and particularly true in the underdeveloped world—was that old pipes and obsolete electrical power sources would cause wildfires, and people would suffer illness and epidemics because of the decaying infrastructure.

These issues persist as long as our government ignores such overwhelming disasters caused by climate change and worn-out local infrastructure. It is seldom cost-effective to replace pipes in our small towns and larger cities. Government's problem is the same issue that the large owners of refineries faced. The public and private sectors can ignore the graying of America only so long.

CHAPTER 8

HIGH SCHOOL DEBATER

By age thirteen, I had become really agitated about this "wrong-side-of-the-tracks" problem. I began to promote to my parents the idea of moving across town. Mom had learned about programs at the Houston Jewish Community Center (JCC) and she drove me there—fifteen to twenty miles—to get an orientation. I remember our first attempt at checking out this new environment. We drove up to the modest brick structure on Houston's Alameda Road. I promptly opened the passenger-side door to lean out and vomit. I was frightened, or at least out of my class, I thought.

But the JCC was a new world for this young teen. There was basketball (a "biddy league" for those under 5'5"), a fine snack bar and some welcoming new friends. Fifty years later, I barely remember Kenny Hart, a painter's son in Jacinto City, or Billy Burrows, whose father worked in the nearby shipyards. They had befriended me, but at biddy basketball I met the first of several guys who would become my lifelong pals.

Introduced to these fellows, I doubled up on what turned out to be a successful campaign to get my folks to consider a move to Houston's more affluent environs. Like millions of families in the 1950s, the Jagodas purchased a fancy place with three bedrooms in a highly promoted new suburb called Meyerland. The house we bought, with its prime location a few blocks from what turned out to be one of the nation's best high schools, was something of a dream come true for me.

Mom and Dad bought the house from a guy who had just won a pot of money on the professional golf tour. He was Jackie Burke, but that golf champion's name meant nothing to me until many years later when I took up the sport. What I remember from that time is how filthy the house was when we moved in. I can still recall fried egg remnants plastered around the fancy electric burners on the stove. After we settled in and cleaned up, I was proud and excited to be in the neighborhood, in part because about twenty percent of its residents were Jewish.

The high school in our new neighborhood was Bellaire. At the time, federal money was just becoming available for highways and, as we moved to this desirable upper-income suburb, also coming along was the loop around Houston, the original part of what today is a complex spaghetti web of highways. But the roads were nothing compared to the amazing educational tracks at Bellaire.

I quickly jumped into the school's journalism class, which would lead to reporting assignments for the school paper, a periodical called *The Cardinal*, named for our high school mascot. I soon heard about Bellaire Debate, the school's champion debate squad. So I enrolled in a speech class that led to my trying out for the debate team. My successful acceptance was a hit, an adventure that further helped change my perspective on life.

Symbolically and materially, these extracurricular activities showed that I was finally among the growing middle-income family class of pre-baby boomers. Kids my age were just two years ahead of the baby boomer demographic that became an important part of American life after WWII, and lasted into 1964.

While there were good teachers at Bellaire, with a curriculum aimed at students on a pre-college track (a positive first for me), Bellaire Debate was especially formative. The debate coach, Mollie Martin, was particularly important. In her early thirties, she was an aggressive speech teacher with roots in Oklahoma. But the main thing about Mollie was that she wanted her people to win debate and speech tournaments. Among the techniques used to foster competition—though then seemingly humorous—was the division of the debate class into two sections, one for the Jews and the other for Gentiles. Mollie also imposed memorable requirements on us, insisting, for example, that we each read the works of Ayn Rand, the famous objectivist whose "individualism" I later came to realize was part of the backbone for American selfishness. At that time, however, Rand's books seemed to me to be just well-written stories.

Mollie's teams almost always won tournaments and, during my high school years, many of my colleagues won individual national championships. Though I was certainly not a star, I did win a couple of trophies as well.

Saul Jagoda debate parent and community leader
Credit: Collection of Barry Jagoda

Our own Bellaire tournament was one of the country's most respected debating tournaments. Two footnotes from this period: My dad found time to raise money to support the tournament, and he was also chosen as the Texas statewide president of B'nai Brith, the national Jewish cultural and philanthropic organization.

Many of my Bellaire classmates went on to become leading scientific researchers, neurosurgeons, important consultants for industry and government, as well as influential lawyers, mostly in the realm of public service.

One close friend from those years, Eugene Keilin, an incredibly bright lawyer-financier, is often credited with helping to save New York City during its financial crisis of the 1970s. In more recent decades, Eugene's spouse, the New York City attorney Joanne Witty, spearheaded a movement to create Brooklyn Bridge Park, turning that shabby large space into a wave of green. When I asked Gene how Joanne had accomplished this amazing feat, his reply was, "Read her book!" Indeed, a contribution to the environmental and political life of the city is encapsulated in the volume, *Brooklyn Bridge Park*, written by Joanne and a co-author, published in 2016.

Another Bellaire High debater and old friend is an Oklahoman, Stephen Jones, who we all called "Bunky." Decades ago, Bunky visited Karen and me in our Georgetown home. Always one with what seemed like an important statement, Jones said then, "Well, Jagoda, it is time for us to get into the history books!" As it turned out, Bunky more than lived up to this pronouncement, as he served as defense attorney for the Oklahoma City mass bomber Timothy McVeigh. Many others of my high school colleagues became civic leaders in Houston and Texas, including some whose footprints ranged globally.

Our highly competent school principal, Harlan Andrews, was the brother of the Hollywood actor Dana Andrews. Like the title of the book later written about French restaurants and cooking, by Joanne Donsky, another classmate, we were the best—*La Crème de la Crème*. But even the best have skeletons in their closets.

One of our young debate colleagues, Kenneth M. Schwartzberg, was incensed that he had been overlooked for the traveling squad to several tournaments. Kenny decided this was because of a scandal. He told me that he and his dad, Gene Schwartzberg, went to the Board of the Houston Independent School District and argued that our debate teacher was playing favorites because she was romantically involved with a member of our squad. I could not then, nor now, verify these charges or rumors, but, within a few weeks, Mollie resigned her post.

She moved to New York City and eventually took a teaching position there at Hunter College.

I did much miss Mollie's teaching, and even her occasional scolding. In retrospect, she was profoundly influential for me and for a generation of us in Bellaire Debate. For example, Mollie directed us to learn, in depth, all sides of what was one year's national debate topic, about federal aid (or control) for local education. This is a hot topic even today, on Capitol Hill.

At a much more mundane level, Mollie had always insisted that her debaters participate in the Tulane University tournaments, because a trip to New Orleans would offer the chance for Houston kids to experience cuisine beyond the ordinary Texas fare. At the time, provincial Houston offered very limited menus, although there were already a few expensive, high quality restaurants, places where a diner could get something besides chicken-fried steaks and other basic dishes.

I remained also involved at the JCC, joining the B'nai Brith Youth Organization (BBYO) in its Houston Cyrus Adler AZA chapter. BBYO is a national Jewish teen movement based in Washington, DC with hundreds of local affiliates. This became my new home-away-from-home, and by the time we were high school seniors, I had won leadership posts in this organization, eventually becoming president of Cyrus Adler, or what we called from the Hebrew, *Aleph Godol*.

In this high school group, I gave a speech saying we were living "in the good old days." Even today, more than sixty years later, I stand by this exhortation. Our group was comprised of some of the best and the brightest of our little Houston Jewish community, and my leadership role gave me confidence that has stuck with me.

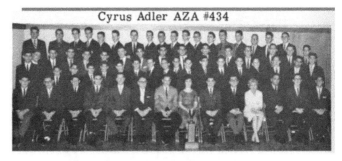

Cyrus Adler AZA, Barry Jagoda, center, outgoing President
Credit: Collection of Joel Loeffelholz

Each group chose a "sweetheart," and ours was the lovely Bobbie Smith.

The summer before our high school graduation year, I was able to practice a concept new to me: "Get your foot in the door." Somehow I had gotten the attention of the guy running the press box for Houston's new major league baseball expansion team, the Houston Colt 45s. My job at Colt Stadium, a venue which two years later was demolished to make way for the Astrodome, was to direct a crew of kids who helped transport the sports reporters, with their typewriters and other gear, up a considerable number of stairs to the press box. One of these young fellows in the crew was Joe Siff, who to this day is a civically minded Houstonian. He has, over the decades, remained a friend. I had a similar job with the new pro-football expansion team, the Houston Oilers, where the food in the press box came from Houston's best local "black barbeque" joint.

Growing up among these folks prepared me to get out into a wider world with a new sense of myself. Although I had failed to take full advantage of the college preparatory environment at Bellaire, I did get along. Turned down by Ivy League schools and deciding that the quality private Northwestern University, in Evanston, Illinois, would not be the best expenditure of my parents' still-meager bank accounts, I chose the University of Texas, in Austin. At UT, the cost of tuition for a year was still just $100.

CHAPTER 9

UT AND JFK

B esides being UT freshmen, almost all the 10,000 students
entering that year belonged to some club or extracurricular
interest group. Some lived in huge dormitories and made
friends there. Others pursued clubs where they could ply their hobbies.
All the religious denominations had student programs. Several
thousand of my fellow classmates joined fraternities or sororities. One
good reason for that choice was to get a better place to live and to
eat than the undistinguished dorms. In addition to the Greek cliques
that often featured beautiful girls and attractive guys, some of us were
rushed by the Jewish groups. At UT, there were about five Jewish
fraternities and about the same number of Jewish houses for girls.

As an independent-minded freshman, I had decided to go
it alone, getting a room at a commercial dorm named the "A-Bar
Hotel." One big survival advantage I had was that my mother sent
along with me a case of tuna fish. That was in 1962, but even now,
tuna salad remains my favorite food.

Kenny Jacobs, another self-actualized freshman from the Houston
Jewish community, took this same move for independence and
ensconced himself at the A-Bar. Kenny became a lifelong friend, and
I was proud of him when he eventually developed into a respectable

saxophonist, living and working as a professional musician in New Orleans and San Francisco.

The A-Bar dorm manager was Winnie Sapp, and she was unexceptional except for her name. I guess I was unexceptional, too, because I now only remember the crucial freshman English class, where we had to start essays with a thesis sentence or face flunking the class. It was one of a few gateway classes that were especially rigorous and intended to weed out unmotivated freshmen. Hundreds, in fact, did fail out.

English was not so hard for me, but I was lucky to have passed algebra. At the same time, loneliness began to set in, and the guys at Tau Delta Phi fraternity were trying to get me to join. This house had the Jewish students with the best grades and, in the previous year, one of their members had been elected president of the entire UT student body. I looked up to two top student scholars, Ronnie Eastman and Ronnie Cohen, who were also Tau Delts, and they became role models for me. So I left A-Bar and moved into the fraternity house.

The craziness there—demeaning fraternity initiation and pressure to conform—was not for me, even though I did become a full member. I left the frat house after one semester but maintained numerous friendships I had made there. Among them was my close high school buddy, David Horwitz, who became an excellent filmmaker and, to this day is a lifetime pal.

I stayed close to a couple of other guys, some from high school, who were attending Houston's superb Rice Institute, later named Rice University. They were already working on the college paper, *The Rice Thresher*. When the White House announced that President Kennedy would be giving a speech at Rice, I got a press pass from my pals. Of course, it promised to be an event not to be missed.

When the press corps and the presidential spokesman Pierre Salinger arrived, I gestured to Pierre where he might sit. Most of the audience was focused on the presidential announcement that our country would go to the moon within a decade. But my attention was on Salinger, who, as I explained earlier, then told me to give him a call when I got to Washington, since I would be searching for an internship that coming summer.

I did drive up to the nation's capital in the summer of 1962, but Salinger never accepted my phone calls. Fortunately, the office of Albert Thomas, then a congressman from Texas, helped me get an internship in the office of Robert T. Griffin, the boss of the General Services Administration. The top guys there were Kennedy retainers from Boston. This was my first exposure to a government that could work for the people.

My next years at UT were an improvement. Eventually finding a nice house, on a street improbably named Happy Hollow Lane, I was able to recruit two guys as roommates who helped pay the rent. They were also distinguished as having run against each other, two years before, for freshman class president. The loser in that contest, Richard L. Cohen, as I wrote earlier, became a treasured, lifelong friend.

The 1963 semester had hardly begun when I ran into my first real brush with history. The White House had announced another trip by President Kennedy to Texas. Most everyone—young and old—can remember where he or she was around noon, November 22, 1963. That night there was to be a big dinner at the local municipal auditorium. To get a dinner ticket, I had phoned a classmate Ronnie Earle, whose father was chairman of the Texas Democratic Party and very close to Texas Governor John Connally. Ronnie's dad would officiate at a unity dinner. President Kennedy was trying to bring together the conservative Connally with two other prominent politicians from the Lone Star State—the liberal Senator Ralph Yarborough, and Vice President Lyndon Johnson.

After finishing up a Friday late morning Portuguese class, I stopped by the offices of *The Daily Texan*, the college paper where

I had been occasionally writing and reporting. The editor asked if I would be willing to attend the unity dinner to get some backstage color to go with the main stories about Kennedy's trip. Delighted, I accepted the press pass and phoned Ronnie Earle with news that I no longer needed to bother him about a dinner ticket. "They shot John," screamed Earle, referring to the governor, as soon as I got him on the phone. "And they may have gotten Kennedy also," he added, referring, of course, to that fateful trip to Dallas where President Kennedy was assassinated. To this day I have the press pass, "The President's Trip to Texas," framed on my office wall.

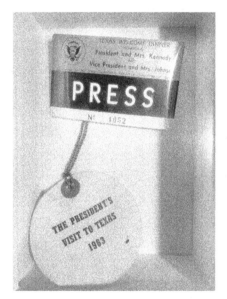

Jagoda press pass, President Kennedy's trip to Texas, November 1963

Credit: Collection of Barry Jagoda

I had spent a previous summer at home in Houston going to the local university and taking a course called Anatomy and Physiology for Nurses. This was my way of getting around the required difficult biology course at Texas and, sadly, bypassing a good introduction to Darwinian science. This was a good example of *corner cutting*. I would continue this sort of foolishness in the coming decades.

Having gotten most required courses out of the way, I began to take college much more seriously. My decision to major in American Studies meant the privilege of having as my advisor the Pulitzer Prize-winning historian, William H. Goetzmann. He later was to be on that White House committee that President Carter had me establish to select a new head of the National Endowment for the Humanities. Goetzmann had been an inspiration: he argued against conventional historical academic wisdom and suggested instead, in his prize-winning book, that the American West had been settled by scientific technocrats—surveyors and engineers—from the US Army, rather than by traders and trappers.

At UT, many of my fellow students and I joined in the local civil rights movement, marching and protesting segregation at a popular restaurant. I am almost embarrassed to report also that our Happy Hollow Lane home was the site of a party we threw for the LBJ White House press corps. They had followed the new president to his vacation White House near Austin. With a roaring fireplace in the background, and many of our friends—and numerous coeds— present, we threw a memorable Christmas celebration which was attended by famous names in journalism. They included Dan Rather and the *New York Herald Tribune* star reporter Douglas Kiker, among other White House correspondents.

My last two years at UT were idyllic as I was consumed by reading, thinking and speculating about the state of the world. The main result of this formative period was a decision that I would not join the Texas establishment, which also meant abandoning plans for law school. There was just no way I'd become part of any government structure—even as a lawyer—if government could promote something like the American war in Vietnam.

Instead, I dedicated myself to shining a light of truth on government malfeasance. I would try to become a professional journalist, hopefully an investigative reporter. To pursue this career, I applied to and was accepted for further study at the prestigious

Graduate School of Journalism at Columbia University in New York City. I had finally made it to the Ivy League.

Our graduating class at UT was 8,000 strong. The commencement speaker was President Johnson who had become increasingly unpopular due to the escalation of the Vietnam War. The president was met by a sizable anti-war protest outside the hall. But the protesters did not get in the way of the pride that was obvious on the faces of my mother and father, my sister and her husband, Bill Nemzin, and my beloved grandmother Rachel.

Our graduating class had included Lynda Bird Johnson, the president's eldest daughter. She had, in our political science classes, been a stalwart defender of her father's policy of bombing and punishment of the North Vietnamese.

I was ever more convinced that I'd have nothing to do with the establishment that brought Agent Orange and mass killing strategies to Southeast Asia. I graduated with an even stronger sense of myself.

CHAPTER 10

COMING OF
POLITICAL AGE

As a college student in the early 1960s, in the peak of the Cold War, I sensed the dangers of being tarnished as an extreme leftist, though my own experience was more theoretical than real.

I did vaguely remember that, inexplicably, my dad had taken me to West 26th Street in New York City to meet Gus Hall, then the chairman of the Communist Party, USA. I must have been about eight or nine. Many years earlier, in the 1930s and 1940s, Hall had been a friend of my father's, when Daddy, a fellow progressive, was working in Ohio to organize unions and liberals. As previously noted, my dad was never a member of the Communist Party, but he was as close to being a sympathizer as you could otherwise get. My mother, Dr. Anne Fradin Jagoda, was also not a party member, but she was pretty sure that capitalism would be replaced by humanistic socialism. As I have mentioned, their idealism would affect my life forever.

I guess these ideas were just fine—at least in a free society—but I was getting a dose of Marxism at the very time that all the other kids in my lower-middle-class suburb were focusing on such mainstream activities as Sunday school and church.

Imagine having somehow to try to reconcile Vladimir Lenin with Jesus Christ while still being in elementary school! There was a good solution: Avoid all these ideologues and try to be a good American kid. The way that worked out was that I inherited my parents' idealism, but the surrounding culture flattened me out into something much more conventional: a political moderate.

A different and helpful role model was my dad's younger brother, Uncle Harry Jagoda, who was a baby when he arrived as an immigrant in New York City, with his mother and my father. Eventually, they all realized they could do better by migrating farther west, to Ohio.

Uncle Harry was one of the family members I most admired.

In Youngstown, my grandfather's family settled among Yiddish-speaking, welcoming relatives. After high school, and with relatively lucrative work, my uncle Harry Jagoda was doing quite well and helping to support his parents, to say nothing of having numerous girlfriends.

All this changed with the Japanese bombing at Pearl Harbor. Uncle Harry immediately enlisted in the US Army for the World War II fight against the Nazis. There, he quickly rose to non-commissioned officer status. For the rest of the war, Sergeant Harry Jagoda served in Italy in the 15th US Army-Air Forces, under the command of General Mark Clark. The top American officers there quickly came to appreciate Harry's talents in many areas of military endeavor, particularly in the quartermaster corps. Sergeant Jagoda, given relative freedom, could just about take care of any problems that might arise.

In Italy, with his relative military flexibility including his own personally assigned Jeep, Sergeant Jagoda came upon the Kabilio family, Jewish refugees from the internment camps that had been set up in the islands of the Adriatic Sea. Prior to the war, they had come from the Balkans, in Bosnia-Sarajevo to Zagreb, Croatia, seeking a better education for their daughter, Flora, already an exceptional musician. She had a lovely voice and played the accordion, which at the time was called a harmonica.

Wedding of Harry and Flory Jagoda
Credit: Collection of Barry Jagoda

Luckily, the beautiful teenager saved her family from the Jew-hunters of the time by constantly playing her musical instrument and singing. The family was moved from camp to camp, eventually ending up being repatriated, under the command of the Americans. There, Sergeant Jagoda discovered the musically talented Flora. It was not too long afterward that there was a military marriage.

After the war, the whole extended family came home to Ohio. Even with her Sephardic and Ladino-speaking background, Flory (Flora's new name) knew not a word to communicate with Harry's family of Yiddish speakers. Shortly, Harry and Flory moved to the DC suburbs of Virginia. There she became a music teacher, while Harry first ran a deli and then—for many decades—was a successful homebuilder. In Northern Virginia, Harry and Flory raised a talented family of four kids. One of my cousins, Andy, eventually became a prominent emergency medicine physician in New York City.

Aunt Flory also excelled beyond her work as a neighborhood music teacher. She would become known worldwide as one of the leading musical interpreters of the Balkan Sephardic culture, whose *Ladino* is a language that combines Spanish and Hebrew.

Hundreds of thousands of Ladino-speakers had been expelled during the Spanish Inquisition of the late 1500s and landed in the regions bordering all around the eastern Mediterranean. Flory became recognized as an important carrier of this fragmented but unique musical heritage, as a composer and arranger of new Ladino songs. She gained fans and adherents around the world, many buying her numerous albums and CDs.

In 2002, Flory received a National Endowment of the Humanities fellowship and was recognized in a special Library of Congress concert. There she was accompanied in the presentation by her children, especially Elliott, the most musical, and Betty (now Betty Murphy), along with her youngest, the very creative Lori and Lori's husband Jeremy Lowell. The always-modest Flory said, "I'm just very happy that I'm being recognized as a composer and a singer of this music."

Barry Jagoda and Adlai Stevenson, 1960 Democratic National Convention

Credit: Collection of Barry Jagoda

For my own part, in 1960, I had worked my way into a job for a Houston radio station, as a reporter at that year's Democratic National Convention in Atlantic City. That convention became notoriously violent as civil rights protests erupted. Former party nominee and previous Illinois Governor Adlai Stevenson had lost out that year to Jack Kennedy. But Stevenson found time for an interview with me and a photograph of our meeting.

But my biggest debut splash came in March 1967 when I was quoted on the front page of *The New York Times,* in this case regarding secret undercover CIA financing of American youth and student organizations.

This quotation about CIA funding was a real jolt because apparently it was true, though it was a shock to me when I learned more details within a day or two. I had been helping another former University of Texas college buddy, James D. Fowler, who had been chosen to head up The United States Youth Council, which was representing the Boy Scouts and numerous other non-student groups at the United Nations and at conferences around the world.

CIA money was indeed flowing to The Youth Council, as well as was funding for a college student analog, the US National Students Association, for *Encounter* magazine, a liberal monthly, and for some labor unions. Leaders of these entities kept the secret to themselves, using the money for their organizational operations. The justification—in the Cold War period—was that the Soviets were doing the same thing with their own parallel organizations. Among leading young recipients, funding was still then kept a secret, apparently even from Gloria Steinem who would go on to become a famous feminist iconoclast.

But the investigative magazine *Mother Jones* disclosed the secret payments and ran a story, although I had not seen it. When reporters at the *Times* saw the piece, they began asking questions. When I told Fowler about the inquiries, he said, "We can't tell the paper much, if anything, but I can now let you know that we had been nearly completely funded by the Agency."

Whatever was the full and eventual truth of the story, which the *Times* had brought to national attention, there was one more part of the saga associated with my help for Jim Fowler, a marvelous, personable guy who died of natural causes in 2011.

My student military deferments had now expired, and I was ready to enter the workplace, so I was a prime target for drafting and induction into the military. But like millions of young men at the time, I came up with clever excuses for not being drafted into the Vietnam War. I was passionately opposed to this conflict and the American role in it. Thus, I had no moral compunction against taking a letter to my draft board in a building on San Jacinto Street in downtown Houston.

On letterhead, Jim Fowler wrote, "To Whom It May Concern, Barry Jagoda is working with the United States Youth Council representing our country at the United Nations." He went on, and concluded, "We ask that Mr. Jagoda be deferred from the draft in the interests of American national security." Of course, the board was pleased to honor this request and provided me with a two-year deferment. When the lottery system for the draft kicked in, I drew a distant number and I was free forever.

From those times at the Youth Council, completely apart from CIA politics, and my great relationship with Jim Fowler, I also developed several lifelong friends, other guys who were also unwitting about the financing. They included the quintessential New Yorker, Michael Glass, a Harvard trained attorney who served in the Carter Administration and later taught at Fairleigh Dickinson University in New Jersey.

Joe Fallon was another New Yorker, from the Bronx, who had superb political instincts. Some years later, I got a phone call from an excited Joe: "Hey Barry, I've just heard a Queens politician at a rally. He is unbelievably good. Let's keep an eye on him." The politician in question was the then-unknown Mario Cuomo, who, indeed, did go on to become Governor of New York, and spawned a very talented family including a son, Andrew Cuomo, who also now serves as New York governor. Another son, Chris Cuomo, is one of our country's more talented broadcast journalists, probing and reporting for CNN.

The scholar in our group back then, and now, was David L. Rosenbloom, whose book, from his PhD dissertation at MIT, *The Election Men*, described the emerging bunch of political consultants— the force behind many, if not most, successful election winners. But Rosenbloom decried the tendency of these consultants merely to serve as hired hands and then to fade away, rather than accepting responsibility to help govern alongside the leaders they had helped create. This was not the pattern followed by David himself, who had helped elect a mayor for Boston, the terrific Kevin White.

David then went on to be chief of staff for White's re-election campaign, and stayed to serve as Boston's Commissioner of Health and Hospitals for more than seven years. Rosenbloom, as a prominent political science professor, worked at Brandeis University, then at Boston University School of Public Health, where he taught and became a specialist in addiction science. David married Alice Richmond, a *magna cum laude* graduate from Cornell University with a degree from Harvard Law School.

Though I still think of myself as a First Amendment purist, I had learned a great deal about how the press and government can be manipulated.

Of course, beneath the surface there are many news stories that could captivate the public's attention, many still untold—for example, the machinations of Donald Trump and his crowd. But as President Trump has said, "I could shoot someone on Fifth Avenue, and nobody would care."

As I wrote earlier, the buddies who helped me witness President Kennedy's visit to Houston's Rice Institute to announce plans to go to the moon, were the editors of the *Rice Thresher* college paper. They went on to amazing careers, and in many cases, expanding the frontiers of American journalism.

Their first move was the creation of the highly respected *Texas Monthly* magazine, styled on city service publications such as *New York* magazine. The theory there, proven totally successful, was that Texas with its more than twenty-five media markets and numerous large cities could be sold as a statewide advertising and journalism vehicle. As those who follow media trends know, this award-winning magazine has long thrived. I was named a contributing editor and made a few small contributions.

We were the first wave of beneficiaries of what was being called *The American Century*, rising from the suburbs to pinnacles in New York City, Washington, DC, Los Angeles and many locations between and far beyond. Of course, I trailed along, eventually outgrowing journalism—so I thought.

Texas Monthly Founding Editor William D. Broyles eventually did move on from this regional orbit to go national and international as editor-in-chief of *Newsweek*. He was the personal choice of *Washington Post/Newsweek* owner Katharine Graham.

One fine afternoon, in Washington—as we drove up Pennsylvania Avenue–Bill, visiting down from *Newsweek* headquarters in New York City, offered up a truism. "There is so much history here!" If the lines of fate had been drawn slightly differently, Broyles, the most dynamic young public person I knew, could perhaps have been president instead of Donald Trump.

Few things anger me more than Trump's continuing assault on the media and his mantra of "fake news." He has called the media "the enemy" of the people and even treasonous for exposing his own unscrupulous and illegal behaviors. His attacks on *The New York Times* have been unrelenting.

In this regard, I particularly want to mention how much I agree with the trenchant comment of my graduate school buddy, Leonard Levitt, who is probably the best American police reporter still writing. He keeps an eye on the New York City Police Department with his weekly, *NYPD CONFIDENTIAL.*

Not long ago, Lennie told me, "We'll know the country is really in trouble if the *Times* goes down!" Right he was, and though some have worried about the frequent investigative tilt in the editorial pages of *The New York Times,* I have always been totally impressed with the integrity of that great paper.

Ever since I came of voting age, I have rarely missed an issue of the daily and Sunday *Times*. Of course, the *Times* is one of the two or three most important publications on the globe.

Thus, as I have suggested, my blood boils when I hear from the current occupant of the Oval Office, frequent references to "fake news," mainly when an outlet carries something with which he, in his wisdom, might disagree. His use of that outrageous and disgusting term, almost always when a news outlet carries something factual, has done much harm to our country, and to worldwide free expression. Trump consistently endangers the lives of journalists who are out there doing their jobs, telling truth to power.

As everyone should know and remember, this "fake news" wording is used only about legitimate news stories that Trump dislikes! I am reminded of the oft-quoted Thomas Jefferson declaration, "If I had to choose between a free government and a free press, I would choose the latter."

But anyone who has looked into the topic knows that our first elected national leader, George Washington, did not want to run for re-election because of the devastating criticism leveled upon him by the opposing party's press. In that sense, Trump is nothing new. So here, Dear Reader, is an answer. For the moment, we will leave *Mr. Tweet* stewing and foaming. Very often Trump, in his crudely deceptive way, smirks and says, "We will see." So be it!

PART III

JOURNALISM

CHAPTER 11

NEW YORK CITY
AND NBC NEWS

Operating on the foot-in-the door principle, I got up to New York as soon as possible after my University of Texas graduation. A place to live in the already quite expensive city was provided by a first cousin who had long occupied a family rent-controlled tenement apartment. Cousin Carl Briseno was a longshoreman who had accepted a government grant to move to the seaport of Mombasa, Kenya, to instruct dockworkers on the latest techniques.

Taking over this three-bedroom fifth-floor walk-up pad on the Lower East Side, I was thrilled at the $60-per-month rent. And to make things even better, I had found a terrific job as a desk assistant at NBC News, where I planned to work during the summer before starting my graduate work at Columbia in the fall. This was wonderful, even though my hours often were from midnight to 8 am and the job, really as a copy boy, entailed not much more than getting coffee for the writers and producers, and efficiently tearing and delivering news copy off the constantly churning AP and UPI machines. Most important for me was that this was a place to meet everybody on the staff, and to add NBC News to my résumé.

During the three-month internship, I got a couple of breaks. First, I had exposure to key decision-makers who learned that I was going to journalism graduate school and would likely come back asking for a job. Second, for the first time I experienced something that, over a lifetime in the news business, would provide amazing satisfaction—getting a real scoop!

The initiative in question pertained to the Texas tower shooting. A little background: On August 1, 1966, Charles Joseph Whitman, a former US Marine and sometime student at the University of Texas, climbed the clock tower on the school's campus and began firing on innocents below, killing seventeen and wounding thirty-one people. These facts are well known to anyone who followed what became one of the first mass murders in our country's history.

Less known, then only to a handful of my NBC News colleagues, was how I provided our network radio operation with an eyewitness to the tower massacre. The killer had gotten up to the top of the tower's 26th floor observatory and was firing away from that location. Only two floors below was the office of one of my former professors, William Arrowsmith, widely recognized as a leading interpreter of the Greek classics. Who could better tell our radio audience of the shootings he saw!

When it was over, I learned that a close buddy and former roommate, Richard Cohen, was one of those who had taken shelter from the attack. Preparing to accept his Rhodes Scholarship (a first from the University of Texas at the time), Cohen, walking on campus, below the tower, after studying in the library, ducked, got lucky and was unharmed. But irony was there to be observed. At the base of the tower were Apostle John's words from the New Testament, "You shall know the truth and the truth will set you free."

In my excitement, I could not avoid the thrill of congratulations from my fellows at NBC News. This was the first time an extremely cynical notion echoed: "Too bad for the dead and dying, but what a lucky break for a journalist." Shame on me for this lapse of ethical perspective, but the idea was to come back numerous times over the next decades as I finished J-School and got hired at NBC News.

During that brief first summer at NBC News, sometimes I had an opportunity to escape my mundane wire-room assignment, including participation in covering local and regional news in and around New York City. Occasionally, I was a member of the news-reporting team headed up by the late Gabe Pressman, who was the epitome of the no-nonsense professional in local broadcast journalism. Even today, nearly fifty years later, I remember the dialog between Gabe and the amazing, persistent City Editor at WNBC-TV, Bob McCarthy.

"OK, Gabe, good morning and I want you down right soon to sweep City Hall," would come McCarthy's raspy voice over the radio band reserved for NBC. "Got it Bob, we're on our way and will give you quick feedback, but don't forget that I need time for that (unspoken by name) investigative project we've got in our sights."

Then we were off into the streets of New York City—our leader, Gabe Pressman in a news car packed with gear, plus a soundman and a lighting technician—and the wowed up, wound up, but fully focused Barry Jagoda, an intern soaking it all in.

This was local broadcast journalism at its peak. The goal then, of course, as loyal readers will appreciate by now, was to *shine the light of truth on the powerful.* Bob and Gabe were always on deadline, trying to be first with political and other stories, mostly with a focus on wrongdoing by elected officials. I could also see that they were sometimes even willing to "get it right," leaving others to be first. This became a lifelong lesson for me as a professional journalist. For me, this was the big time, and by any objective measurement, BIG TIME it was!

Gabe brought to life the great professorial cliché I would later hear from our influential graduate schoolteacher, John Hohenberg. When we asked what to do if we needed more time to finish a running story (perhaps a tight election with the polls still open),

"GO WITH WHAT YOU'VE GOT," would Hohenberg intone. This is what reporters still do. Professor Hohenberg, who died at age ninety-four in the year 2000, was the author of the seminal book, *The Professional Journalist.*

In later years broadcast journalists could cover the news single-handedly, or perhaps with one cameraperson in a crew. But I will never forget what my mentor at Columbia J-School, Fred W. Friendly, has called the main requirement during this period of newsgathering: "a thousand-pound pencil," referring to the weighty gear required by broadcast journalists of the day. Friendly had come to academia after resigning as the otherwise influential president of CBS News, in a dispute over coverage of congressional Vietnam War hearings.

It was through Fred's intercession that I got down to Washington to interview Senator J. William Fulbright, a leading opponent of the Vietnam War. Based on interviews and work around the senator, I got the material to write my master's thesis, a study of the Gulf of Tonkin Resolution. That legislation allowed President Johnson to use military force against North Vietnamese communist troops in Southeast Asia without receiving from Congress a formal declaration of war. I am proud to say that my thesis is still to be found in the library collections at Columbia University.

There were many others on the faculty at the J-School, but one who was also very influential for many of us was Mel Mencher, a distinguished former journalist who authored *News Reporting and Writing.* This book that not long ago passed through its 12th edition, insisted that students always dig deeper while reporting a story. In that sense he was, for us, a precursor influence that was later appreciated in the work of Robert Caro, well-known as a biographer of the powerful. Caro says that he learned from his own city editor at *Newsday,* to "keep turning the pages," to get to the bottom of potential malfeasance. But these important journalists and teachers never made a student or reader feel comfortable, because that was not necessarily the function of reporters.

Other professional lessons came at formative periods in our lives as future journalists.

After finishing graduate school, I was offered a news position at NBC, as a junior writer mainly for local news, though the assignment rotation frequently landed me as a writer to help prepare news segments for the dominant morning TV *Today Show*. This all happened less than a year after my arrival there (in another piece of luck) when a strike by NBC's news writers propelled me to the network's Washington bureau. As I was heading out the doors of the New York newsroom, I expressed concern—fear perhaps— about the unusual assignment to be a writer-editor in the nation's capital. I mentioned this trepidation to the famous NBC News correspondent Edwin Newman, for whom, not much more than a year earlier, I had delivered wire copy so he could write his daily midday network television news program.

Newman gave an unforgettable response. "Well, don't worry because this strike is a mini-crisis and could provide a real chance for you to move ahead." Looking at me kindly, Newman added a piece of institutional history: "General Sarnoff once told me, 'A crisis gives the individual room for great progress.'" David Sarnoff, the founder of NBC, had been dubbed "The General" after the Army named him a Reserve Brigadier General of its Signal Corps in 1945.

So, in early 1968 I was sent off to the nation's capital to my second real job in journalism. Though my ambition had been to keep politicians honest, the job at the NBC News Washington bureau was much more prosaic.

I had become a desk editor of correspondents' daily news copy, primarily for radio news on the hour, or "hourlies," as they were called, even though I had just gotten out of journalism school within the past year. Although I wasn't going to do much stylistic editing of the scripts presented by David Brinkley or even Nancy Dickerson or Richard Valeriani, and the other famous NBC News correspondents, they all welcomed my flagging an occasional factual error in their news copy. Back then, during each day even the most important broadcasters took their turns at sending out, for the NBC Radio Network, these five-minute newscasts, many of which originated from our studios in Washington.

The part of the job I loved entailed assigning correspondents and film crews. The boss of this process was a hardened, thoughtful editor named Christie Basham, the chief Washington assignment editor. Early in the morning, or late in the day, when Christie was not on duty to make most of the significant assignments, the several of us who took our turns "in the slot," gave directions which were almost always followed by the NBC News reporters and camera crews.

I developed further confidence and pride after being asked to help cover big stories on location on Capitol Hill and at the White House. I later realized that this initial work as a young Washington newsman would in later life help me understand a good deal about the interplay of politics and the press. That sort of "on-the-ground" training is invaluable.

This Washington experience would lead to what my boss, the compassionate Len Allen, the bureau's assistant news director, said was "my first big scoop," and he later gave me his notes of what had happened.

One afternoon, my old high school debate buddy Stephen Jones, then chief of staff to a Republican congressman, called me very excitedly on the telephone. Jones said, "Jagoda, get the network, Ike is dying." It turned out that an intern in the congressman's office was a granddaughter of former President Dwight Eisenhower, and they had gotten advance notice.

Running into Len Allen's office, I related this "news." Allen asked, "How credible is your source?" I replied, "I trust him; he wouldn't mislead us."

"Okay," said Len, "Let's go with it. Get a mobile unit rolling and send crews and correspondents to Walter Reed [Hospital]!"

As a result, NBC News had a few hours of advance notice on this momentous news of the day. I still have Len's notes of the afternoon, congratulating me. This story gives an idea of how establishment our coverage was back in those days.

But late one day, when I had come to work as that evening's Washington "desk assignment editor," the red phone, the urgent line from New York, buzzed. Of course I grabbed it.

"Who is this?" demanded Reuven Frank, executive vice president of NBC News. I knew his voice—he was at the top of the management chain. "Did you see that wire story about the sheriff down in rural Virginia, reported dead?" asked the boss from NBC News headquarters in New York. Before I could take another breath, Reuven added, "Get a correspondent, a crew and charter a jet to get down there!"

Well, to make a long story short, along with a top general assignment correspondent Robert Hager, we jetted to this tiny town to find that the sheriff had committed suicide. "Not much of a story here," the correspondent reported back to New York.

But of course, we had that jet and that crew and me as producer. The clock was ticking, and the general assignment budget was getting spent. "But," said the experienced NBC News correspondent, "I'll file a piece for the *Today Show* and we can release the jet because we can get back to Washington commercially."

Now there was a useful lesson: We took a good, quick look and that was that. Impressive experience for a novitiate!

Most important, however, for me was that I also was about to get a chance to help in coverage of the emerging Apollo moon-landing program.

My big break came during this period when NBC News needed a junior writer to man the overnight watch of the first in the series of the Apollo manned space shots. Somehow, I got the call from Executive Producer Jim Kitchell. As a result of this part-time, add-on assignment, my name had come to the attention of an executive producer at CBS News.

Congressman Bob Eckhardt on bike in 1969 with note of thanks to Jagoda

Credit: Collection of Barry Jagoda

But while I was still in DC, there was a personally meaningful interlude. A hero of my university days, a liberal Texas politician named Robert Christian Eckhardt had just been elected to Congress from Houston. When he got to Washington, I helped him out. It was my first political gig. In future years he always reminded me that I was his first and best media advisor, having let him know precisely how to land an interview spot on the *Today Show*—then, as now—a coveted outlet for reaching a broad swath of the American public.

Bob, a dedicated environmentalist, always rode his bike to his office and meetings in DC.

I did worry if I was crossing the line from my job as a responsible journalist, but if any politician could then have been worth it, Eckhardt was. He was always a great man, in my book!

CHAPTER 12

CBS NEWS: APOLLO 11 AND WATERGATE

After numerous interviews with the executive producer of the Special Events Unit at CBS News and his two main assistants, senior producers—all very important news coverage leaders—I was hired as an associate producer on the team that would prepare for Walter Cronkite's coverage of the space program. So, it was back to New York and the top of big-time broadcast journalism.

The job was to get further and fully *read-in* on coming plans to land astronauts on the moon. Meantime, we were also subject to multiple assignments in the Special Events Unit. This was the group that covered the big breaking stories including political campaigns, conventions and election night, in addition to the Apollo moon mission.

Robert Wussler, as executive producer, was also an extremely talented hands-on newsman whom CBS News had selected to manage the huge budgets, the many hours of airtime and a cadre of producers and top correspondents for big stories. He was focused now particularly on the Apollo program which had been designed to carry out Kennedy's promise. But before we could get a man on the moon, we had to mobilize for a worldwide solar eclipse, for earthquakes at home and for various global crises.

Also, as mentioned in the introduction to this book, I had been assigned by CBS, on behalf of all the American TV networks, as pool producer for the summit meeting between President Gerald Ford and Soviet General Secretary Leonid Brezhnev. This event took place in the far east reaches of Soviet Asia, near the port city of Vladivostok. The summit, focused mainly on arms control, was said to be successful and the America coverage went smoothly. However, as the meetings ended, I was directed to get across the Russian continent—crossing, by rail, eleven time zones, traveling on the Trans-Siberian Railway—to Moscow to settle up with Soviet television for their cameras, broadcast booths and other assistance in the American coverage. On this, the longest railway line in the world, my passage took almost a week. I mainly remember sleeping most of the way, and arriving in the Soviet capital somewhat refreshed. We were able to quickly agree, with mammoth Soviet TV, on what we owed.

I had been provided a room in the Hotel Rossiya, a lodging with more than 3,000 rooms, then the world's largest hotel. It was adjacent to Red Square, its twenty-one-story tower looming over the Kremlin walls. Earlier, from at home in New York City, I had gotten a communication through to my mother's brother, my Uncle Louis, who had come to the US as a boy but later, as an optician, went back to Moscow to help build communism.

As I stood on the front steps of the huge hotel, I could see pedestrians walking up, including Jacob and one of his two daughters, my first cousin, Aliya. What I now remember was the shock of seeing this young woman, at her father's side, who appeared to be a nearly perfect likeness of my mom, her American aunt. We had a pleasant family reunion before I had to fly home to continue my work at CBS News.

One of our more sober—but also somewhat amusing— assignments was coverage, including live television coverage as warranted, in the county seat of Edgartown, Massachusetts for a news story titled "The Inquest into the Death of Mary Jo Kopechne." She had drowned in a car accident at Chappaquiddick Island on July 18, 1969, while a passenger in a car driven by Senator Edward Kennedy.

The sordid accident knocked the Massachusetts Democrat out of the presidential race after it was learned that he made a limited effort to save the young woman while saving himself. They had been coming from a party celebrating "the boiler room girls," the women who phoned to supporters during a Kennedy re-election campaign.

During the courthouse deliberations, we were standing-by with our live cameras at the ready, in case a verdict was announced. (Kennedy pleaded guilty to leaving the scene of an accident that caused bodily harm and was set free.) While waiting, I took a call on the "hot phone" connecting us with the broadcast center in New York. It was our boss, Vice President for News Coverage Gordon Manning. I much liked and appreciated Manning. He had a previously successful long career in shaping news coverage, included editorship of *Newsweek*, and decades at CBS News and later at NBC.

In this call, however, I was embarrassed when Gordon said he had noticed some costumed impersonators walking the streets around the courthouse. "Hey Barry," said Manning, "How about some pictures of that Bobby Kennedy look-alike out there?"

"Well," I responded to the boss, "we've seen those clowns, but they certainly don't merit any attention, do they?" Immediately Gordon said, "Aw, c'mon, Jagoda, put some tabloid in your blood!"

I've never forgotten that little exchange, which may say much about the urgency in TV news for ratings. Of course, we sent the picture back to New York and it actually got used as a tiny piece of coverage in *The CBS Evening News*.

The only fringe benefit of the emotional Kennedy assignment was the splendid fresh lobster rolls at the airport snack bar in Chappaquiddick.

During that summer of 1969, coverage plans for Apollo moved into high gear. We began to focus on all the astronauts. I interviewed the famous Alan Shepard, who was the first American in space and subsequently was to land on the moon in 1971.

Astronaut Alan Shepard with note inscribed "To Barry Jagoda with personal regards and thoughts of the good old days!"

Credit: Collection of Barry Jagoda

Still, the main attention was on the July 20, 1969 planned moon landing by astronauts Neil Armstrong and Buzz Aldrin. Soon after being hired by CBS News, I learned that my main assignment was to be the top producer—the breaking news chief—at NASA's Manned Spacecraft Center (renamed the Johnson Space Center in 1973) in Houston.

Within a few months, after many trips between New York City and Houston, I had gotten to know many of the key players at NASA, including most of the astronauts. Along with such colleagues as the experienced CBS News correspondents Bruce Morton, Steve Young, Morton Dean, Bill Plante and others, we would be ready for anything—including a safe moon landing, or a disaster.

Astronaut Buzz Aldrin on Moon: inscribed "To Barry Jagoda With the Best Wishes of the Photographer Neil Armstrong, and signed also "To Barry Jagoda with Best Wishes Buzz Aldrin"

Credit: NASA

In a strange way, the historic and exciting events of July, 1969—including the launch of Apollo 11 from Cape Kennedy, the thrilling moon landing and the safe return of Armstrong, Aldrin and their team member Michael Collins—became almost just another news story for me, though of course a really unforgettable one. Here again was that cynical view, "fine for the participants, but another chance for a journalist to get ahead!"

The loftiness of my position at CBS became boomingly clear one day when I was in the Washington bureau. While there, I encountered one of the all-time important bosses in television news, also not one to make anyone particularly comfortable: William J. "Bill" Small, the fearless, and fearsome, Washington bureau chief.

One day when I first had been ordered down to Small's domain at 2020 M Street, N.W. in Washington, Bob Schieffer had also come aboard for duty. Schieffer was later to become CBS News anchorman and star. Today the boss was showing the neophyte around: "Here," said Small, "is the desk of Dan Rather. That is Roger Mudd's cubicle. Over there is Marvin Kalb." These were all in the pantheon of the globe's top broadcast journalists. After the tour, Schieffer asked, "Yes, sir, but where do I sit?" Small replied, "Schieffer, your desk is out on the street doing some reporting!"

I traveled in those circles when I was assigned to help cover what came to be known as the Watergate scandal, the type of story that had inspired my desire to be a journalist. The story broke before Richard Nixon was re-elected to a second term as president. Many of the top journalists covering the White House knew Nixon was in trouble, but we all were struggling to prove what was initially just whispers of presidential hush money and burglars.

My assignment was as the second producer on Nixon campaign coverage. Bob Mead had been Dan Rather's main producer, but the network always geared up with extra staff for campaign coverage.

When I came down to Washington to get started, I had an introduction to Rather's always ready, always aggressive approach. "Okay, guys," he now said to our team, "do you have your dimes on hand?" I had known that the most critical part of covering a president—

after getting an accurate story put together—was the "death watch:" waiting for an accident or something worse. Rather would never let opposing networks get out in front of him watching and covering the president. The dimes worked in any pay phone, in case of tragedy.

Earlier, Rather had gotten in trouble when he had a confrontation with Nixon, in March of 1974. It was at a news conference at a broadcaster convention—coincidentally in Rather's (and my) hometown of Houston. Typically, when called on at news conferences, the named reporter rose and mentioned their name and affiliation. But when Rather stood there came applause from the audience, local reporters mainly, but also a few of the members of the traveling White House press corps. In response to the surprise clapping, before Dan could ask his question, President Nixon, who liked to throw reporters off balance, smiled and issued an immediate rebuke.

"Mr. Rather, are you running for something?" To which Rather quickly replied, "No, sir, Mr. President. Are you?"

Dan Rather questions President Nixon
Credit: White House photograph

This came during the period leading up to Nixon's eventual resignation. Eventually Rather was able to ask his question, a tough inquiry about recent findings of Special Prosecutor Leon Jaworski concerning the Watergate investigation, which contradicted some statements by President Nixon and his White House. Thus, it was this back-to-Nixon moment from Rather that is enshrined in the photograph above, subsequently signed, "To Barry Jagoda—who when times were tough was there, helping. From his friend and admirer, Dan Rather."

But Nixon's continuing efforts to mount a defense faded away as it became more obvious that the President was in serious hot water over the break-in at Washington's Watergate Hotel, then headquarters of the Democratic Party. After months of denial, White House tapes were discovered making clear that Nixon had ordered a special unit to spy on his Democratic opponents.

Our group was assigned to produce special coverage re-enacting Nixon's words and slurs on the Oval Office tapes, which were so damning to the president that it led to his resignation instead of a certain impeachment. Under new Executive Producer Russ Bensley, within hours we had organized producers and correspondents for this job. I was extremely proud to be part of this production, which eventually won an Emmy Award. One more example of "too bad for the perpetrators but great for the journalists."

Emmy Award for coverage of Watergate, 1973-1974, Russ Bensley, Executive Producer, Barry Jagoda, Producer. May 1, 1974

Credit: Television Academy of Arts and Sciences

For several years afterward, we remained at the ready for big stories while also getting more Emmy nominations. Meantime, my former boss, Bob Wussler, who had led our coverage of Apollo 11, had gotten promoted to run all of CBS's operations in Chicago, making it a first for a newsperson to gain a big-time overall corporate position like this. "Bobby," as everyone called him, eventually became president of CBS Sports, directing coverage of several Superbowls, and then helped Ted Turner found CNN and other media enterprises. I have always had great respect and appreciation for Bobby, who passed away of natural causes in 2010.

The 1976 election cycle would soon arrive, and by then I had been elevated to the rank of senior producer at CBS News. It was a very good job, but I was pretty much unable—in these big deal assignments—to use my journalism training for spotlighting government malfeasance. Except for Watergate—and that was a big exception—my work had become fairly routine and predictable. I was ready to move on.

CHAPTER 13

NEW MEDIA ADVENTURES

A first attempt at getting beyond the strictures of network television came along with my formation of a new company, *American Television Alternative*. It was 1975 and we would start a fourth network offering a superior quality product, not standard network entertainment fare.

Along with numerous other critics, I'd been concerned about some otherwise excellent television organizations—often at the level of local news—who substitute what might be considered good judgement for a focus on accidents and minor events because of the availability of eye-catching film and video. In my opinion, the chasing of ratings had also allowed this practice to creep, occasionally, even into otherwise excellent network news broadcasts, and even more so with the widespread availability of "picture" from amateurs and others who post on social media.

In my view, a better model for good news judgment has come from the mostly advertising-free *NewsHour on PBS*.

So, I had begun to think about alternatives for news and public affairs programming, but perhaps with a sufficient, but limited, amount of advertising. Conversations with several service-oriented advertisers led me hopefully forward. *Variety*, a daily and weekly publication—then, as now, with bellwether coverage of television—ran a front-page story, with a banner headline reading, "JAGODA EYES FOURTH NETWORK," including full background of the idea. This was before expansion brought three cable news networks, before ESPN with its full-time sports coverage, or even prior to Fox with a fourth broadcast offering.

Several months of exploration suggested there might be light for such an idea, but it was at this moment that a couple of old college buddies made me an offer that, at the time, I could not refuse.

These good friends were operating a successful advertising agency and public relations agency in Dallas and they wanted to expand to Madison Avenue. Seeing me as the perfect vehicle for this expansion to the traditional home of the advertising and media business, I was offered a post as a full partner in what became *Houston/Ritz/Cohen/Jagoda,* announced by a logo that we soon plastered over the huge window of a five-story building I leased at Madison Avenue and 65th Street.

The idea was to develop and produce new approaches to television and public service media. Now definitely ready to move on from my successful career at CBS News, I found this idea to be a most interesting entrepreneurial venture where I would not be alone in new approaches to media. Now divorced after a five-year marriage to a woman I had met at CBS, I was free to be seduced by this opportunity.

Moving into three of the floors of the Madison Avenue building, we got started on New York-based projects. The first very successful assignment was for philanthropist John D. Rockefeller III, who wanted to commemorate the founding of America by setting up a television and print media program for reflecting the thirteen-year period from the Continental Congress to ratification of our Constitution.

Then we thought to produce an opera, *Aida,* at La Scala in Italy. This was followed by a plan to bring major league baseball to Cuba, with a return series between Cuban and American teams in the United States. One of our agency partners was a huge opera fan and another—fluent in Spanish—wanted to improve US foreign relations using baseball diplomacy. We came close to success, as seen in the news coverage below from *Sports Illustrated* and *The New York Times.*

Sports Illustrated covered our Cuban baseball plan.

Cuban Baseball Diplomacy
November 24, 1975. "Cuba, Sí. Baseball, Sí"
Credit: Sports Illustrated

Below is an excerpt from the SI piece:

By William Leggett

Although there was a time when major league clubs regularly played exhibitions in Havana, the last professional baseball game there involving teams from the U.S. and Cuba was the nightcap of a doubleheader between the minor league Rochester Red Wings and Havana Sugar Kings 15 years ago. A local curfew forced the game to end in a tie, and soon thereafter worsening diplomatic relations between the two countries compelled the Kings to move to the U.S. They completed the 1960 season uninspired and unwanted in Jersey City, N.J.

For weeks now reports have been circulating (SI, Oct. 27) that a group of major-leaguers would fly to Havana next March to play two games against a Cuban all-star team, and that at least the first game would be televised in this country over ABC. Last week these reports were confirmed; now only administration approval is required to make the visit official. That is expected soon, perhaps this week.

Almost as surprising as the prospect of the game itself is the fact that the trip was neither conceived nor organized by the State Department, baseball or the network. It was put together by a pair of 31-year-old independent TV producers, Barry Jagoda of New York and Richard Cohen of Dallas. They worked on the project for more than a year, spending about $10,000 of their own money in the process.

Jagoda was with CBS from 1969 until 11 months ago and received an Emmy Award as one of the producers of Watergate: The White House Transcripts. Cohen, a friend of Jagoda's since the two were roommates at the University of Texas, is a former Rhodes scholar who is fluent in Spanish and currently works as a free-lance writer and producer.

While Jagoda was vacationing at the Austin home of Texas Monthly Senior Editor Paul Burka in 1974, he and his host watched TV news films of Senators Jacob Javits of New York and Claiborne Pell of Rhode Island on a visit to Cuba. They reacted to the telecast in different ways. Since there are no regular flights from Havana, television man Jagoda wondered how the film had been transported to the U.S. Burka said, "Aside from cigars, the big impact if we ever reopen relations with Cuba will be in major league baseball." An intense fan, Burka expressed the opinion that there were as many as 15 players on the island good enough to make big-league clubs.

Jagoda next discussed the notion of a Cuba-U.S. game with Cohen, but the trip remained in the talking stages—a telephone call to Commissioner Bowie Kuhn had drawn mild interest in their project—until Jagoda returned from producing the networks' joint coverage of President Ford's November 1974 trip to Japan, Korea and the Soviet Union. When Jagoda left CBS early this year, he and Cohen decided to head for Havana and make an attempt to interest the Cubans in their idea. A member of Javits' staff told them the way to get to the island was through the Czechoslovakian embassy, and Jagoda and Cohen met with Czech Second Secretary Rudolph Hramadka. They had a 45-minute discussion of sport in Cuba, then Hramadka excused himself and left the room. He returned with a seven-month-old copy of Granma, Cuba's national newspaper. In it was a picture of Fidel Castro attending the 1974 boxing matches between amateurs from the U.S., Russia and Cuba. Circles had been drawn around those nearest Castro in the photo, and Jagoda and Cohen were told those were Cuban officials they should see.

Jagoda called Havana and was surprised at the ease with which he got one of the circled men on the phone. The official quickly gave Jagoda and Cohen permission to fly to Havana. Before they left, the two men again talked to Kuhn. Although he remained interested, the commissioner still did not authorize Jagoda and Cohen to say that they represented the major leagues.

When Jagoda and Cohen arrived in Havana, they found the Cubans wanted to see something in writing. They borrowed a typewriter, sat down under a palm tree at the Hotel Nacional and wrote a proposal off the top of their heads. The Cuban government reacted favorably to it, but gave no firm commitments.

Frustrating months of letter-writing and delays followed before Kuhn flew alone from Pittsburgh one October morning to Mexico City. While the Pan-American Games went on nearby, he met with Jagoda, Cohen and Cuban sports officials in a hotel room, and an agreement was reached to play ball. Kuhn allowed Jagoda and Cohen to offer the games to all three networks; only ABC was interested enough to pay $165,000 for the rights. As organizers of the event, Jagoda and Cohen will pay the expenses of the U.S. team. They will not receive any gate receipts, even though crowds of 60,000 are expected to attend each game. Spectators are not charged admission to sporting events in Cuba.

The only previous games in which top pros have met the best so-called amateurs from a Communist country were the 1972 and 1974 series between the U.S.S.R.'s national hockey team and Team Canada. While those were dramatic events, they had only minor political impact; they were played long after a warming in relations between Russia and North America. The Cuban contests should also be first-rate affairs, but the diplomatic advances that evolve from them may be far more significant.

Alas, our diplomatic/baseball project was a perfect example of a "near-miss." International politics, and then Secretary of State Henry Kissinger, jumped into the way, as reported by *The New York Times* a few months later.

Kissinger Vetoes Cuban Baseball
January 7, 1976. "U.S. Cancels Cuban Baseball Telecast"
Credit: The New York Times

U. S. Cancels Cuban Baseball Telecast

By Les Brown

Jan. 7, 1976

An exhibition baseball series in Havana between all-star teams of the United States and Cuba, which was to have been financed by the sale of television rights to a network, has been called off by the State Department because of Cuba's military involvement in the Angolan civil war against pro-Western forces.

A State Department official indicated that Secretary of State Henry A. Kissinger had been favorably disposed to the plan several months ago, seeing it as an opening wedge in establishing communications with Cuba, but denied approval when Cuba supported the Soviet Union in Angola.

Although the planners of the event, Barry Jagoda and Richard Cohen, still have hopes that a resolution to the Angola conflict might permit the goodwill games to be played as scheduled, on March 21 and 22, the State Department source indicated that the project was dead.

Mr. Jagoda, a former producer for CBS News, and Mr. Cohen, an independent producer in Dallas, had negotiated successfully with the Cuban Government for the games to be played there, with the possibility of a Cuban team later visiting the United States. They then obtained an agreement from Bowie Kuhn, the commissioner of major league baseball, to send a team to Havana consisting of seven players from each of the four divisions of the two leagues.

"Cubans are intensely interested in baseball, and the baseball commissioner's office here, believes there are 19 or 20 players in that country—all of whom are considered amateurs —who could make the big I leagues," Mr. Jagoda said.

Baseball diplomacy with Cuba was to have been a variation on Ping-Pong diplomacy with China, and Mr. Jagoda indicated that his plan was partly motivated by a desire to see improved relations with Cuba, which has not had official diplomatic contact with the United States for nearly 15 years.

He noted too that American baseball would have realized promotional benefits from the exhibition, which would have been played just before the start of the new season.

ABC Sports, which now has the TV rights for major league baseball, had agreed to pay $165,000 for the opportunity to televise the Havana exhibition games in this country, despite technical problems that might have made it necessary to route

*the picture through Europe in order for it to be presented
live here.*

*The complex transmission logistics, which probably would
have involved two trips across the Atlantic for the television
signal, were bizarre in light of the fact that Cuba is only 90
miles away from the Florida coast.*

Thus, the notorious Henry Kissinger had become a foil. As was
typical, his *realpolitik* concerns, based on some facts and some
unproven imaginations, succeeded in holding back, for more than
four more decades, peace efforts between the US and Cuba.

Forty years later, my partner Richard Cohen and I could only
watch from the sidelines as the Obama Administration succeeded
in the US opening to Cuba that we had ardently pursued. This
experience reminded me once again that life is often subject to near
hits, as well as the opposite. I have watched with dismay, in 2020, as
Donald Trump and his anti-immigration administration has made
Cuba largely off limits to US citizens and businesses.

Despite making progress in developing public service television,
our advertising agency ran into problems. The building with its logo,
Houston/Ritz/Cohen/Jagoda, survived, but our partners all had
competing items on their personal agendas. For me, what was to be
an incomparably much more exciting and challenging opportunity,
as we have seen, was simultaneously coming up in the form of Jimmy
Carter and his campaign for the presidency.

Eventually though, even very much more important to me than
Jimmy Carter, was my falling in love with Karen, now my wife of
nearly forty years. Professionally, my exquisite spouse with her
degrees from top university programs brought to our partnership a
keen understanding of technology, logic and productivity. She was,
and is, a one-person IT department, always keeping us one step ahead

of developments that make life bearable in our information age.

For example, one day in the late 1970s, Karen moved into our townhouse some enormous pieces of equipment: a new and advanced Lexitron word processor and a printer designed to replace my old electric typewriter. Since then she has wisely insisted that we stay up to date. This book would never have been even contemplated without the technological advances Karen has continued to bring to our household. She pushed me to create a web site, and is almost always a better resource, these days, than the highly useful "AppleCare," that one-stop telephone helpline.

I am reminded of a remark by the late Jody Powell, who had a splendid mind, and much more than occasional good judgment. We were chatting, early in the Carter presidency, in Jody's office of the press secretary, adjacent to the Oval Office, when Powell trenchantly commented, "If any of us guys can find a woman who will put up with us, we are more than lucky and much more than deserving." So true! In Powell's case, along the way he had found Nan Powell, a wonderful, very smart and amazingly tolerant spouse. Ah, Jody, I miss you, your passion and great skills, even to this day.

PART IV

GOLD COAST AND GOLDEN FRIENDS

CHAPTER 14

BICOASTAL

With Ronald Reagan in the White House, Karen and I decided to become bicoastal. As a result we learned a bit about California, Los Angeles and the Hollywood culture.

The term *bicoastal*, incidentally, attracted the interest of *The Washington Post*, which in 1981 ran an article about celebrities whose work kept them shuttling between the two coasts. Karen and I were mentioned in the piece, as were Jack Valenti, president of the Motion Picture Association of America, and Barry Goldwater Jr., the Republican congressman from California. Goldwater Jr. was the son of the late senator from Arizona who had become the Republican Party's presidential nominee back in 1964.

Karen and I were greatly taken by David Ritz's well-reviewed, sentimental novel, *The Man Who Brought The Dodgers Back to Brooklyn*. Ritz had been another of my college pals, and he was a creative, clever writer. The fantasy he produced was a bonding story about two dear friends from Brooklyn, along with a girl pitcher who, like Sandy Koufax, would not work on Yom Kippur. But in the story, when she *was* on the mound, virtually no one could hit her pitching.

We wanted to turn Ritz's story into a movie, and we decided we'd need to rebuild Ebbets Field brick by brick.

After raising more than $100,000 from friends and from personal funds, we found a home in the Los Angeles's Wilshire District's Windsor Square neighborhood, leased a VW convertible, and were convinced we'd be making a major motion picture.

We made many mistakes, among which was inviting *The New York Times*' Hollywood reporter, Aljean Harmetz, to chronicle our forthcoming triumph. But one year later this was her story: https://www.nytimes.com/1982/01/04/movies/the-110000-blunder-or-the-man-who-couldn-t-work-movie-miracles.html

Hollywood Movie-Making Effort
January 4, 1982. "The $110,000 Blunder, or
the Man Who Couldn't Work Movie Miracles"
Credit: The New York Times

We had eventually been poised, as a fallback, to produce a made-for-TV movie, but could not get the rights and our partnership in order. So we left LA and David, and our dear friend, his wife Roberta, and Karen and I limped back to DC. For their part, the Ritzes eventually became grandparents with a fine large family. David, now an author of more than twenty books, is widely regarded as one of the leading interpreters of American culture, particularly music and the Afro-American experience.

Back in Washington I began a new career in public and marketing communications, which eventually included decades of work as a consultant and activist using new media—first for five years as director of public relations of DC's George Washington University (GWU), then as a Washington-based publicist for Canada's largest technology company and eventually, as Washington director for a worldwide productivity firm.

More than a digression, though, was when I accepted a leadership position at The Raoul Wallenberg Foundation, established to honor the role of Wallenberg—and his entire family—in literally saving European Jews and other refugees during the Holocaust. One particularly central moment for me, as chairman, was putting together a multi-day celebration of Wallenberg's work. We were joined in Sweden by partners in this effort, including Washington attorney Steve Goldman—a man with a finely tuned, exceptional sense of morality—and Robert Walker, an American Studies professorial colleague from GW.

For the event in Sweden we won support from His Excellency, The Dalai Lama, who spent a week with us. This highly unusual honoring came through the professional friendship among the Dalai Lama and other Wallenberg partners, including Dr. Frank Ochberg, known worldwide as the leading authority on post-traumatic stress disorder (PTSD). Friendships gained in this effort have lasted a lifetime.

Meanwhile, Karen, in her role as one of the first hugely successful saleswomen in the personal and business computer field, was chalking up good bucks while becoming indispensable for information technology services among many of Washington's top media people. Not the least of these were star journalists and columnists Hugh

Sidey, Michael Beschloss and Art Buchwald, as well as the owner of *The Washington Post*, Katherine Graham. Incidentally, Mrs. Graham with her huge mansion happened to be our back-door neighbor behind our wonderful Georgetown home.

For me commercial writing, using new media and learning about higher education administration was eye-opening. But after five good years at GW, I began working under the umbrella of the DC area's leading high technology PR firm, Stackig, Swanston and White. The job afforded opportunities to travel worldwide, all over Canada, back to the American west coast, to the Paris Air Show and to high technology and telecommunications conferences globally. This work, which required that I learn more about how to employ new forms of old and new media, probably was a more innovative use of my skills as a writer and journalist than even my earlier work at the pinnacles of broadcasting.

Eventually I moved on to become Director of Communications for IMPAC, a worldwide productivity enhancing company. There, we were in the business of promising corporate owners very substantial cost reductions in their operations by improving processes and other variables.

For me, this work provided another chance to get around the globe, and I traveled to such destinations as Hong Kong, East Germany, England and many other distant locations. I helped IMPAC seek new clients and then often would write success stories for newspapers and websites, even then working more deeply in digital media.

Annually for half a decade, Karen and I would travel to Ireland to help put on an event to commemorate *The IMPAC Literary Award*, with a prize of at least $100,000—the globe's richest—going to an author selected from nominations by libraries from around the world. We loved Ireland and got to travel all over that wonderful country, with side trips to Scotland and other parts of the United Kingdom.

The late Jim Irwin, founder and boss of IMPAC, was extremely generous to his successful employees. He operated out of his mansion and grounds in Litchfield, Connecticut, but set up a spectacular headquarters in Punta Gorda, on the Gulf Coast of Florida. IMPAC's Florida base—with lavish facilities, including training rooms and a good library—was built from the very substantial profits generated by Irwin's productivity consulting business. Punta Gorda became a second home for me, particularly when the winter snows and freezing temperatures made Washington quite unpleasant.

But I still had a hunger for my original craft of journalism and, nearing the end of the twentieth century, I did return to become a travel writer for *The Washington Times.*

My position with the *Times* had many advantages, most particularly the opportunity to report and write at leisure from many countries around the world. I often thought that Walter Cronkite was certainly correct when he referred to television's evening news programs, with only twenty-two minutes for journalism, as merely "headline services." The great anchorman urged citizens at least to read newspapers for more depth and understanding. Traveling to and reporting from a dozen diverse locations such as Croatia, Turkey and Slovenia, for example, gave me a chance to do much deeper reporting.

For instance, working as a reporter and writer again, I gained insight (which I was later able to mine) into a glamorous woman, a beauty queen contestant and fashion model from Slovenia, Melania Knaus. Melania had posed for a *Sports Illustrated* swimsuit spread and could be seen in the buff in *GQ* magazine in 2000. She had attended a year of college at the University of Ljubljana, in Slovenia's capital city, and spoke several languages.

After rejecting several overtures from Donald Trump, a boastful New York builder, Melania married him in a lavish ceremony in Palm Beach in 2004. Within a few years, the Trumps would successfully sponsor the immigration, from Slovenia, of Melania's parents, who then became US citizens.

Slovenia was particularly interesting as it had been one of the six units governed in Yugoslavia by Joseph Tito. During the Cold War, Slovenia was given the role, by Tito, of dealing with the West. Because I was there for two months and assigned for almost the same amount of time in nearby Croatia, I could see how advanced Slovenia had become because of this postwar role, though Croatia was also fascinating with its Adriatic seaports and numerous islands. In one of my stories, I quoted the claim of Hollywood producer and director Stephen Spielberg, that he preferred to cruise along the coast of Croatia because its many spectacular Adriatic islands were never more than an hour apart, making for, he believed, the best private sailing in the world.

My return to print journalism, with deadlines in months instead of TV's instant requirement for constantly producing stories, or within hours, gave me a chance for some real writing instead of just knocking off stuff for a headline.

I specialized in interviewing heads of state, such as the Republic of Georgia's Eduard Shevardnadze, the former Minister of Foreign Affairs of the Soviet Union. With the Soviet breakup, Shevardnadze told me he had returned to his home region of Georgia "to save his country." He reluctantly did agree, when I asked if there were large sums of money involved, "but it was all patriotic," he insisted. I also wrote a story about the Georgian town of Gori, birthplace and childhood home of Joseph Stalin.

In one region of Georgia bordering on Turkey, a real despot was personally taking a substantial cut of border taxes. We wrote about this as well, and it presented a less-than-flattering picture when published in Washington.

But for me, this return to print journalism provided constant learning experiences. For example, I found out that in the plantation economy of Trinidad, there was still a need for field workers, particularly after Britain stopped the slave trade in 1836. No problem: Import workers from Muslim lands.

So this explains why the lovely island nation of Trinidad and Tobago is forty percent Muslim, forty percent African and a mix of other religions. Much has been written about this by the superb novelist V.S. Naipaul, who is known for his comic early novels set in his home country of Trinidad, as well as for his other insightful chronicles of life and travels.

Karen had joined me on a two-week Caribbean vacation in Tobago, which tenderized my two-month assignment there. We stayed on island paradises among rainforests and spectacular beaches. It was in Trinidad's exquisite botanical gardens, set in Port of Spain, the nation's capital, that I received a call on my cell phone from Winifred Cox, head of communications at the University of California in San Diego.

"Would you come to San Diego for a job interview?" she asked. "We have an opening for a director of communications and our committee thinks that your background and résumé make you perfect for this important job," Win added.

This was, I think, what Karen may have had in mind when she had earlier said we could move out to coastal California. All I needed was a job!

Thus, I was recruited for what turned out to be years as communications director for the University of California in San Diego (UCSD). This provided two top-of-the world perks—the splendid weather in San Diego's La Jolla beach community, and an assignment to help publicize scholars who were more interested in their own research, writing and other work than they were in merely getting publicity.

CHAPTER 15

PERCHED IN CALIFORNIA

Returning to the ranks of higher education boosters—this time in the nearly perfect weather environment of coastal California—turned out pretty well for my employer, The University of California, San Diego (UCSD), for me and, eventually, good for Karen, too. I had become deeply engaged with the work of many of the superb scholars at the university located high on the "mesa" in San Diego's coastal neighborhood of La Jolla.

Though UCSD is one of the nation's youngest great universities, it rings up top ratings on most of the measures and assessments of higher education institutions. This is particularly true in the sciences but, as director of communications, I had the chance to focus on the often less heralded work of researchers in the humanities and in the social sciences.

Typically, as scholarly authors would prepare to place research results in the national journals of their fields—sociology or political science or the arts, and so forth—my job was to alert the nation's top reporters. They were almost always pleased to have tips for what would become important stories, often in *The New York Times, or The Washington Post* or the *Los Angeles Times.*

Sometimes we had to settle for such outlets as *The Chronicle of Higher Education* or regional papers around the country, many of which might have a specialist who was very interested in the work of our researchers. It was in this work that I further applied more narrow media channels, such as the emerging social media and the specialized broadcast channels such as C-SPAN and other rising outlets in cable television.

Successful at UCSD, I was able to grow my skills and begin more deeply to develop ways of employing new media and other specialized outlets. We opened our own UCSD television studio to make interviews easier for our scholars. This meant they could be interviewed right on campus, and then quickly get back to their offices or labs. We did not charge the networks extra for this service, which they liked, particularly for the flexibility of getting experts immediately scheduled to go along with their priorities and the flow of the news.

From my new vantage point in La Jolla, I was also able to look back in wonder as our national politics began to change. No longer were political aspirants able simply to issue a press release and hope that some news organization would find the material useful.

At UCSD we would create our own publications using the internet, email and printed newsletters, while also making this material available to reporters who were writing their own stories on their own websites, podcasts and blogs (a term derived from the shortening of *weblogs*).

In her own entrepreneurial mode, Karen Jagoda now continued to develop a media outlet which she had founded in DC, in 1998, under the auspices of E-Voter Institute, where she was president. Examples of their fascinating work were the lively conferences and voter research they conducted. These efforts particularly served to educate about how strategists were increasingly spending more money on the internet for candidates for public office.

By the time Karen started a podcast, *Digital Politics with Karen Jagoda,* in 2007, the money spent online had risen from next to nothing in 1998 to $22 million in 2007. After the successful use of the internet for fundraising and persuasion by Democratic candidate for president Barack Obama, Karen found an increasing audience and wider range of guests for her show. Now, digital enthusiasts are encouraged by predictions that in 2020 campaigns at least $20 billion in advertising dollars will be spent for political campaigns, with an estimated $6.5 billion going to digital media, nearly equal to what will be spent on television advertising.

Also, in response to the plethora of news emanating from the research labs in Southern California, Karen started the *Empowered Patient Podcast*, which became a successful trade resource for those interested in her reporting on the intersection of medicine and technology. I was especially proud of how my wife, this former DC marketing expert and think-tank policy analyst, had developed into such a well-regarded journalist.

The new media also offered an outlet for my journalistic interests, as I moved from full-time work at UCSD to semi-retirement as a contributing writer and correspondent for the new *Times of San Diego*, a digital daily, which had developed a following of several hundred thousand online readers. There I covered professional golf, and worked on stories about political and cultural activities that sparked my interest, such as the local symphony and other civic matters. This included topics such as earthquake alerts, political malfeasance and matters of local—and sometimes national— importance.

Ironically, only after I had moved away from Washington did I begin fully to realize that my interests now were those of a citizen of the nation, no longer much interested merely in the personal machinations of business and commerce.

In a way, this was unfortunate because my family business back in Houston had grown into a huge ship-channel industrial conglomerate, now supplying valuable specialized products and helping their petrochemical corporate clients with work of various sorts. Mr. Jay's little grocery business had morphed first into a scrap and wrecked-car operation, then to North Shore Supply Company. There, hundreds of employees helped provide huge financial returns for my nieces Gloria, Marcia, and Brenda, with their husbands, Buzzy and Stan, who eventually had taken over the company from my sister, Lou Beth and her husband, Bill.

In this third family generation, Gloria and Brenda had earned law degrees. Marcia and Gloria had married exceptionally talented men with advanced degrees in management. Karen and I watched as their progeny developed other interests of their own, in finance and starting up their own companies. This was a test case for seeing how many generations could last in a family business before the later kids—having been given "wings" by their parents—would fly to their own interests, pursuing travel ventures and other personal projects. With the huge wealth that had been generated came a freedom not even dreamed of by my own parents.

When I see the bumper sticker, "Not All Those Who Wander Are Lost," I think of one of these fourth-generation kids named Michael Bluestone, who was to marry a beautiful Houston physician. After college and into his thirties, Michael has been traveling the world as a trip leader for adventure seekers. As a kid he lived in Italy and became fluent in the language.

David Bluestone, Michael's slightly older brother, worked in the giant family business for a while—as heir apparent—but eventually decided to go on his entrepreneurial own. With his spouse, the lovely and thoughtful Marcie, David is raising a beautiful young Houston family.

Another compelling young family guy, my great-nephew, Ben Katz, came to Houston from Wall Street, with his charmingly intelligent spouse, Diana. And there is another family member who I have enjoyed: my great-niece, Marisa Katz. In Houston, Marisa worked for the family business and then married a Minnesotan, Sam Kelner, who has also joined the family company.

Soon, these nieces and nephews had children and grandchildren I have hardly even met. When possible, though, I sought out those primal relationships and tried also to stay in touch with Karen's family in Baltimore. This had included her parents, Doris and Jay, her especially loving grandmothers and her twin aunt and uncle Gloria and Bernard. Karen's sister, Jan Bernhardt Schein, her late husband, Dr. Jay Schein, and their three daughters Hallie and twins Johanna and Chelsea have further anchored us to Baltimore.

I have stayed relatively close to many first cousins—at one point we numbered fourteen, but are now down to ten. I am in regular correspondence with Allan, Barbara and Nan, my first cousins, the adult children of the late Aunt Evelyn Jagoda Solnik and her personable husband, also deceased, my Uncle Carl Solnik.

I did have a feeling of justification for my earlier decisions to leave behind my family and its fortune. For me, getting out of Houston offered lifelong financial loss, and separation from my family. Essentially, I had traded the possibility of real wealth and prosperity to become what I considered a public servant, or perhaps better described as "a citizen of the nation."

Another national citizen is my friend, Victor Emanuel. Growing up in Houston, I had forged a life-long connection with Victor, a wise soul with a passion for politics. But, possibly more important for Vic is his even deeper love of birds and respect for the environment. This led him to found *Victor Emanuel Nature Tours*, universally considered to be one of the very top ornithological operations around the globe. Victor and I stay in close touch via email. When we can, we meet in his operational headquarters town of Austin or some other place around the world. Victor is also one of the leading Texas liberal lights of our generation.

In later life, perhaps not ironically, I've also been sustained by some of my oldest friendships, a couple of guys and their wives, from all the way back to high school: Allen Israel and Jeri, along with Donnie Herzberg and Vickie. About the time Allen was running for international president of AZA (the youth-led fraternal organization for Jewish teenagers), I got to help him in what, only half-jokingly, was my first big national political campaign.

"Izzy," as we affectionately nicknamed Allen, picked up some ancient poetry, updated the verse and instructed us to "Make new friends, but keep the old for these are gold and those are silver." We didn't win Allen's challenging election, but the verse has stayed with me and is kind of a lifelong motto. I hate ever losing a friendship. In young adulthood, I had served in the Israels' wedding party in Memphis on December 30, 1964, and we have stayed close ever since.

Vickie Herzberg, who was in my high school class and was a fellow debate team member, had always been a beauty and still is, now in her seventies. Though she went on to gain a PhD in microbiology, somehow she found time for Donnie, even while he was in medical school.

Don Herzberg is a fine example of a guy who seemed to do everything right. He even studied to gain a master's in literature after he retired as a doctor, and then went on to write some meaningful and memorable poetry. His 2019 work, *Dancer on Earth*, contains haunting thoughts. One little piece, called "Dying Again," is about losing dear ones. Donnie's verses in this book have meant a lot to me, including memoir-type expressions about a constantly on-the-road watch-salesman father and a completely devoted Mom.

We have grabbed memorable reunions with these old friends, first at my 250-acre farm in Virginia, later in New Orleans, and we've sketched out plans to meet soon again. Karen and I, now in our sixties and seventies, relish our chances to get together with these couples.

I refer to my farm, because that is the way I think of the beautiful property of which Karen and I were longtime part owners. Early in 1977, my college friend and political ally, Jan Lodal, decided that we needed a retreat from the tribulations of Washington. He cooked up a plan for us (along with another Washington insider, Fritz Mondale's top aide, Jim Johnson) to buy this wonderful getaway, purposely located just beyond the commuter/suburban zone. It is in Orange County, Virginia, a location just a few miles away from Jefferson's Monticello, and in the very jurisdiction from which arose President James Madison. The place is named *Restless Farm,* and from the front porch, there is a vista, still lovingly implanted on my brain, looking down upon the splendid Rapidan River.

Our farmhouse overlooking Rapidan River in Virginia
Credit: Collection of Barry Jagoda

Another highly respected partner was Elizabeth Lodal, who has won all possible awards as a world-class high school teacher and principal. She is the woman who Jan, luckily enough, snagged as a lifetime spouse and partner.

Jan and Elizabeth were among the crowd that had met when they were in college, at Rice. He went on to become Henry Kissinger's arms control and defense systems expert. In this role, Jan served as a top advisor to the NSC head, who was to become secretary of state for President Nixon.

Later, Lodal was a high government official in the Clinton years. I have always tried to check in with Jan when trying to get some sensible ideas about foreign policy and domestic politics. In my view, a group of us long ago made a mistake by not promoting Jan in a run for Congress from his native San Antonio. He would have brought a lot of wisdom to that body.

Restless Farm gave us the pleasure of meeting two other memorable figures, including the local historian William H.B. Thomas, and an archetypal country lawyer, H.W. "Wat" Ellerson. I spent many leisurely afternoons on the front porch at the farm getting briefed on the rather dense history of President James Madison of Orange County, and of the entire region by Bill Thomas, a man whose numerous books on these topics were engaging. Wat is a civil libertarian with fine passions for automobiles and for keeping an eye on government, not necessarily in that order. To this date, though 3,000 miles apart, Watkins, Karen and I occasionally exchange emails on the evils of the day.

On the other hand, because we were occasional dinner guests of the local gentry, I noticed a cultural tic that went against all I had learned growing up about how to treat people. As we sat in the garden of a local splendid mansion, sharing an aperitif with our hosts, along came the other invited guests. Standing up to greet the newcomers, I was pulled back with, "Let them come to you!" This standoffishness may have been a local feature, but was contrary to my own upbringing. It is a habit we did not mind leaving behind.

Artist depiction of country residence for Barry and Karen Jagoda, Rapidan, VA
Credit: Collection of Barry and Karen Jagoda

Karen and I eventually, but reluctantly, sold our interest in Restless Farm and moved on. Before we got away, though, a great artist and architect of that time, Doug Michels, gave us an alternative farmhouse design, signed *A country house for Barry and Karen Jagoda.*

Doug was a founder of the "Ant Farm Collective," a group that buried ten or more Cadillacs into the ground in West Texas to show off their love for that vehicle's once-famous tail fin. It was a sad time when Michels lost his life on an art trip, falling off a very tall cliff in Australia.

For decades Doug had also been mightily appreciated by Elliott Himmelfarb, my good buddy in DC, and his spouse, Janet Minker. Karen and I called them "MinkFarb." When they pulled up roots and moved to Sarasota, Florida, Elliott built for them a splendid modern residence while Janet, a very talented graphic artist and photographer, became chair of the Sarasota Architectural Foundation. From our geographical distance, we stay in touch.

In DC, for more than two decades, Karen and I had relished our townhome in the perfect inner-city neighborhood of Georgetown. A block away was to be found the unsurpassed gardens at Dumbarton Oaks. On the three-acre grounds across from our 29th Street house was a huge mansion built by Herman Hollerith, who had invented the computer punch card and created the Computing Tabulating Recording Company, which eventually became the IBM Corporation.

Karen agreed to finance a wonderful year of art lessons for me at the nearby Corcoran School of the Arts. Suffice it to say, I was happy enough to learn a bit about color and design in this new endeavor. At the end of our block was a precious chapel on the premises of the historic Oak Hill Cemetery, whose president, George Hill, is our buddy and former stockbroker. We loved our house location so much that, even after we had moved to California, we purchased two spaces in this cemetery.

CHAPTER 16

MAKING NEW FRIENDS

An enduring lesson Karen and I took away from our Hollywood experience, besides the necessity of having an agent, was that the best place to live was adjacent to the Pacific Coast. There the wonderful breezes—at least in our eventual San Diego home neighborhood of La Jolla—kept temperatures generally in the seventies Fahrenheit year-round. For that reason, La Jolla is said to have the best climate in North America. For someone who grew up in the treacherous summers of Houston, this is no small matter.

La Jolla is a strange combination of suburban and urban. This is because of the University of California, the Salk Institute for Biological Studies, and many other leading research institutes that are located in this region. Scientific discoveries there have been an inducement for biopharmaceutical and other high-technology sciences to locate nearby. As a result, La Jolla has attracted an extraordinary collection of well-educated, often interesting neighbors to live in what had once been a mundane 1950s suburb.

What happened in La Jolla is of historical interest. In the early 1960s, the prominent oceanographic research professor, Roger Reveille, convinced both the City and County of San Diego, as well as the famous and powerful Clark Kerr, president of the University of California system, to establish a university. But there was a significant problem. Until then, folks of the Jewish persuasion were informally made unwelcome in these precincts, but, as Reveille is said to have put it, "You can't have a university without Jews." So, Reveille, as part of the deal to establish UCSD, acquired (with help from the Scripps family fortune) enough space to build somewhere between fifty and 100 homes, many with spectacular views of the ocean. These lots were available to anyone who might become a member of the new university faculty family, regardless of religious or cultural persuasion.

Nearly at the same time, a perfectly suited student apartment-housing complex, *Coast Apartments,* was constructed with similar ocean views and made available to graduate and professional students. That community is located two blocks from our home, and well within walking distance to the ever-expanding campus. Since those early days, the student population has grown from a few thousand to more than 40,000. Now, of course, many dozens of other choice housing spaces are available, along with hundreds of nearby commercial apartments.

Thus, most of my neighbors in this unusual suburb ride bicycles, walk or employ skateboards and the like. I could write a newsletter just about what I encounter outside my door. One might bear in mind that we moved here for the weather but came upon a treasure trove of urban intelligentsia.

For instance, canvassing against President Trump with one of my neighbors, who has both a medical degree and a law degree, we thus helped to turn this part of Southernmost California from John Wayne Republicanism to a place where reasonable politicians could seek and win high government office. This is an example of citizens taking back their own political affairs. Along with another neighbor, a UCSD oceanography professor, we were proud to help elect to Congress the environmental-focused attorney Mike Levin as part of the anti-Trump sweep in 2018.

Our street, La Jolla Farms Road, was once a place where an affluent Texas cattleman ran his herds. When UCSD acquired this property, the university sold parts off to buyers who erected multi-million-dollar oceanfront homes, replacing the cows. We were very lucky to find one of a few remaining architecturally significant cottages, overlooking the Pacific. This has made an extremely nice choice for us and our dogs.

Our exceptional La Jolla residency came about, instead of having to purchase a normal San Diego home, because Karen insisted that I have a short commute to work, staying off massive Southern California freeways. What had been my longtime UCSD La Jolla office, incidentally, overlooked the world-class Torrey Pines Golf Course, made especially famous by Tiger Woods' tournament triumphs there. More important for me, as a semi-retired regular hacker, is that in less than a mile, I can get from home to a golf nirvana where I pay a pittance in residential green fees.

From my high school days, I had been close to Ronald Cohen who has been influential to me all these decades because of his wisdom and values. Though Ronnie, a very fine lawyer, died suddenly of a stroke in 2016, I still communicate with his former law partner, Bill Small, who has set up some fine golf outings for us over the years. Another UT buddy, retired psychiatrist and psychoanalyst John Bannister, is a guy I stay in touch with by kibitzing about golf and our college days. Along with his wise spouse, the recently retired clinical psychologist, Pamela Yu, they live at the Oregon coast.

Meanwhile, with regard to playing golf, one of my main two hobbies, I was fortunate to hear about something called UCSD Casual Golf Club, and for the past fifteen years have joined upward of sixty mostly delightful souls in special tournaments all around the vast San Diego County. When I was a new hire out here, I knew this would also be a good way to learn the geography in one of the nation's largest counties. That has proven to be the case.

In our La Jolla neighborhood one can hardly walk a dog without learning something new. We have been blessed with two extraordinary canines, first a Cairn terrier named Charlie (who lived with us from eight weeks of age until his brain gave out at 18 years), then an amazing Jewish/German mini schnauzer named Timothy Otto Jagoda. As Timmy and I take our three daily walks (keeping "spry," as my creatively close buddy from Columbia J-School, Alan Adelson, had predicted), I have to be sure to get in some dynamic stretching each morning or Tim will walk-run fast enough to make my limbs hurt.

Over the past nearly two decades, in addition to helping me stay in relatively decent shape, these inquisitive dogs have aided in my natural reportorial instincts. By now I suppose I've met hundreds of very interesting students, teaching professors and researchers. Often, as Tim and I walk along paths adjacent to the Pacific Ocean, we might engage in conversations about mutual areas of curiosity.

Charlie, the Cairn terrier, used to hate skateboards and their riders. Timmy seems to enjoy everything, particularly when he is allowed to stop students, and others, to be petted. Turning this suburb into a splendid urban neighborhood was not something Roger Reveille necessary planned on, but it is a great example of unintended consequences. For instance, these days, when we stroll past a UCSD distinguished professor of mathematics, I normally greet him with "Have a reasonable day." The charming, optimistic prof invariably replies with "Have a spectacular day!" And most often, we do.

When I first came to La Jolla, my curiosity and professional assignments were mainly in the areas of the social sciences and humanities, fields in which I had before then read widely, if not deeply. Now I have learned almost more than I can stuff into my poor brain about neurobiology, chemistry and physics. My neighbors have been good conversational teachers.

One neighbor, now a retiring distinguished professor in the neurobiological sciences, has been my squash racquets partner for fifteen years. I treasure the friendship and workouts with Bill Kristan (William B. Kristan Jr.). Bill also loves dogs, but probably no more than does his spouse, Kathy French, also a PhD researcher, who has for twenty years found time to help manage the UCSD chapter of Phi Beta Kappa.

As I've noted, some psychologists say it is very difficult to make lasting friendships later in life, but in La Jolla, we have disproven those theories. Among our other new and dear friends from La Jolla are the prominent scientists John Sedat and Elizabeth Blackburn. She is a Nobel Laureate and president *emerita* of Salk Institute. Both John and Liz refuse to join the ranks of the retired. John, well recognized for his discoveries, is closing in further on the use of advanced microscopy to peer into the nucleus of a cell. Liz is in constant demand worldwide as a speaker and lecturer as she promotes a greater role for women in science. She is also leading an international movement for collaboration among scientists, particularly as research funds have become less available.

John, always extremely modest, just as he was when I first met him on the sidewalk by the corner of my home, mentioned that he had taken a leave from his own laboratory in San Francisco to accompany his wife to here in La Jolla "for a job." That post turned out to be presidency of the Salk, where she held one of the most important scientific management jobs on earth. Typical of John, he modestly, called it "just a job." Liz's Nobel Prize came for her discovery of important adjuncts to chromosomes, called *telomeres*. In case you want to know more about this subject, ask Liz (if you happen to meet her), or just read her 2017 book, *The Telomere Effect: A Revolutionary Approach to Living Younger, Healthier, Longer*, co-authored with psychologist Dr. Elissa Epel.

My most constant neighborhood companion, also a dog walker— but his, like those of Queen Elizabeth, are of the Pembroke Welsh

Corgi breed—is the retired biological specialist, Gary David. With his wife Denise, they are both splendid, very well-read neighbors. We first met when Gary introduced me to the concept of *overreach*, or *overbuilding* by UCSD into the neighborhood. But, as it turns out, most of the nearby magnificent canyons and leftover eucalyptus groves have remained nearly virginal. We love these wild spots that are within blocks of our home! This coastal California living is the true legacy of our attempted movie-making foray into Hollywood.

When I began to think of myself as semi-retired, I first cooked up a news blog called *At The Top Journal*, which actually drew some readers to my personal reflections on politics and culture.

In more recent years, my journalistic addiction has been satisfied by work as a contributing writer for the very popular online *Times of San Diego*, (www.timesofsandiego.com). There, with the indulgence of Editor-in-Chief Chris Jennewein, I write about music and politics and environmental matters, or most anything that seems important. Some of my time is taken up preparing news stories about the fabulous La Jolla SummerFest, one of the nation's leading annual music celebrations, or the excellent San Diego Symphony. I'm also able to report and write about advance earthquake preparations, or on a variety of other topics that may catch my attention and curiosity. Because of Jennewein's years of experience as a newspaperman, *Times of San Diego* is managed in a way that has become a wonderful outlet for my newsman instincts as I continue a lifetime as a professional journalist.

Some of my neighbors send me articles of their research from scholarly journals. Just the other day, president *emeritus* of the University of California, my friend Dick Atkinson (Richard C. Atkinson), mentioned a reference to his academic paper from the 1960s, now reprinted for a fiftieth anniversary remembrance of this seminal work on memory. This is not atypical. A regular lunch partner is Stephen Reed, visiting professor of psychology at UCSD. With Steve, whose rigorous theoretical mind is currently focused on cognition and the organization of information, I have spent hours chatting about books, including Marshall McLuhan's influential contributions.

The 2007 didactic book, *This Year You Write Your Novel*, by a prolific writer himself, Walter Mosley, particularly intrigued me. His prescription: Start every morning writing for at least four hours. Keep that up for six months or more, and then tear up the manuscript you have produced and start over. Mosley argued that after those arduous hours, you *might* have a manuscript that could be fit for sharing with a literary agent. Ah, what discipline!

CHAPTER 17

KEEPING OLD FRIENDS

O ne college classmate who I have long warmly appreciated as a musical organizer and artist in his own right, Richard "Kinky" Friedman, never followed anyone else's rules. As soon as he came back from a Peace Corps stint in Borneo, out came *Sold American*, the first of many albums released by *Kinky Friedman and The Texas Jew Boys*. That record included such lyrics as:

Faded jaded falling cowboy star
Pawnshops itching for your old guitar
Where you're going, God only knows
The sequins have fallen from your clothes.

Another brilliant production from Kinky and his troupe had the song element, "We Reserve the Right to Refuse Service Unto You," which combined Friedman's satirical concerns about anti-Semitism and civil rights. I can still hear a line from those songs, "Congregation on the nod, just the chosen folk doing their weekly thing!" As Kinky's southern/Jewish/country music reached wider audiences, his group toured the nation and successfully took their act worldwide.

One fine week, Karen and I were in New York City when we visited Kinky in his loft residence. He had decided to expand his cultural offerings to a detective novel, which became the first of dozens of such successful fiction outputs. I had been dubious way back then, but, as on so many occasions, Kinky would never let conventional wisdom stand in his way.

Country music star Kinky Friedman
Credit: Collection of Barry and Karen Jagoda

Before he was widely known as "Kinky," Richard Friedman and I first "collaborated" in helping to win the election in 1965 of Gregory O. Lipscomb as president of the UT student body. Pre-Kinky had an old red pickup truck that he drove around promoting Greg's ultimately successful campaign. As a result of being on the winning team, under the principle of "to the victor go the spoils," Greg made me head of stump speaking at UT. One time we had the distinguished writer William F. Buckley there to be picked on. Buckley may not have expected this event as part of his duty as a scholar-in-residence, but he was a good sport.

Greg has been a friend for more than fifty years, through his work as an assistant to California's Governor Jerry Brown, through his marriages, through his expertise in federal communications policy, and now, as he works again from his base in Austin.

But, if Kinky were to be at one pole, at another pole would be one of the most responsible journalists of my close acquaintance, a great friend over many years, Robert Feder. Almost always correct and appropriate, Feder has been reporting on media in Chicago for more than forty years. As an insightful critic with a devoted following, Rob is a continuing force to be reckoned with by Windy City media.

In what would have to be considered a storybook friendship, Feder first came to my attention early in my career at CBS News.

One day I got a communication from him, then a cub reporter and high school student in Skokie, Illinois. Feder was starting up The Walter Cronkite Fan Club, a project surely the great anchorman would look at askance. But instead, Walter was delighted! Every year on Cronkite's birthday, the Club—make that Rob Feder—would send along a necktie to Walter, and damned if the great journalist would not wear this tie as he broadcast *The CBS Evening News* to an audience in the many millions.

Way before Feder had completed studies at the excellent journalism school at Northwestern University in Evanston, Illinois, he had created, for hundreds of members of the *Cronkite Fan Club*, a regular newsletter and outreach program. All these antics could have masked Rob Feder's superb skills as a writer and reporter, but the club president went on to be a star at the *Chicago Sun-Times* and later was a not-to-be missed online journalist.

And, I suppose, one could hardly argue with the much younger Feder that if you were going to have a hero in the field of journalism, Cronkite would not be a bad choice.

Another lesson that came my way was from the incomparable storyteller, Gay Talese. Working for the *Times* and for *Esquire* magazine during the 1960s and beyond, he helped to define literary journalism. As a reporter, Talese said he would "gather string," pulling together matters he had observed or thought of, later turning all of that into award-winning stories.

Of course, there have been many books about New York City, but none as charming as Talese's first work, *New York: A Serendipiter's Journey*, published in 1961. In this volume the mannequins are brought alive, as are the nighttime office cleaning crews, showing what makes New York the place that it is. Talese wrote that New York had 5,000 prostitutes and 200,000 stray cats, along with other fascinating facts. Not only did this superb writer have a wonderful curiosity about everything around him, but he also knew how to turn observations into compelling tales. Among his many other books, my favorite is *The Kingdom and the Power: Behind the Scenes at The New York Times, The Institution That Influences the World*, written in 1966.

I have been trying Talese's method in this book of recollections and commentary, "gathering string," sometimes which just turn into jangles. But, of course, as Talese knew, and as I know, every writer needs an editor to keep the yarn manageable.

In my life of meeting most unforgettable characters, one was a guy named William Paley. This was not Chairman Paley, the giant who founded CBS, and ruled over the New York City skyscraper known as Black Rock. "Our" William Paley, Billy, was Mr. Paley's son. Along with Billy and others, Karen and I started up a disco for preteens called *Little Feet* in the Virginia suburbs of DC. After a few months we knew we had another near-miss on our hands and closed the operation. But Billy has remained a friend. One time, as he and I were sitting around relaxing, he happened to look down at my decent pair of shoes. "My dad once told me you could always gauge the quality of a person by the shoes they were wearing," Billy offered.

For some reason, that one-liner reminded me of another adage, this one by the very distinguished writer and reporter Marilyn Berger. She had a story in *The New York Times* saying you could tell how rich a man was by the number of times he changed clothes daily, from PJs to smoking jacket to workout gear, to business suit, to evening wear, etc. There may be something to that story, though Berger was at that time the spouse of Don Hewitt, CBS News' all-time most famous and most skillful producer and the creator and executive producer of *60 Minutes*. He was living in the Hamptons at the time, a haven of the privileged.

Mentioning the name of Don Hewitt reminds me of one of the stories reported by Sally Quinn in her 1975 book, *We're Going to Make You a Star.* There, Quinn wrote that I, along with another young CBS News producer, Mark Harrington, had saved her in London from being bedded by Hewitt, by moving her away from the production crew hotel to a safer overnight location. We had all been assigned to produce live coverage of the wedding of Princess Anne. Sally was to anchor alongside one of the great remaining "Murrow Boys," CBS News correspondent Charles Collingwood. The broadcast turned out pretty okay, but I've always remembered how difficult it can be when you are thrown in as an amateur, as was Sally, into a big-time job in live television.

Eventually Sally, a good print reporter, returned to her original outlet, *The Washington Post*, where she did, in fact, develop as a star, writing for *The Post's* innovative popular section called *Style*. I have had many friends who were *Style* writers, not the least of whom was Annie Groer, a pal since we had literally met as teenagers when I was an intern in DC.

Sally married the most famous newspaper editor of our time, the *Post's* Ben Bradlee. Ben had written and edited many important stories, but the Watergate exposé work of Bob Woodward and Carl Bernstein was the one he would be remembered for. Their names and deeds were enshrined in *All The President's Men,* the book and movie that the public and many journalists most often remember as the Watergate scandal.

As I think back further about great writers of my acquaintance, there are several more who were close friends and graduate school buddies. Paul Wilkes had gained many awards for his book and television series, *Six American Families*, about the lives of American families of varied geographic and socioeconomic situations. Among his more than twenty books is Wilkes' own memoir, *A Catholic Life.* Paul's recent, very interesting contribution is *A Second Career*, in which he urges all retired folks to find meaning in something different from their main profession. Paul certainly did that. After journalism, joined by his skillful wife and partner, Tracy, they have established up to twenty orphanages throughout India for young girls.

Earlier I wrote the name of Leonard Levitt. He is one guy who will probably never stop investigating, reporting and writing, until even when he almost functions from his tomb. Lennie—in between creating novels and producing *Conviction,* the award-winning volume about an alleged Kennedy family murderer—has been writing about New York City cops, off and on for almost sixty years. This police reporting, now NYPDConfidential.com, started even before we had graduated together from journalism school.

Among my most endearing friendships was with Susan Irwin and her one-of-a-kind spouse, Dr. Harold Kaufman, trained in the law and in psychiatry. We had first met in 1976. Susan was photographing the Carter campaign and, along with many others, we were working to elect Governor Carter. Possibly the longest lasting value of that successful 1976 presidential campaign, for Karen and me, was our deep friendship with Susan and Harold.

This is no small thing for, as our mutual buddy, Washington celebrity dentist Dr. Ted Fields first observed to me many years ago, making new and deep friendships in later middle age is not easy. But, in Washington and beyond, I have had decades of exchanges with Teddy and Suzanne Fields, a conservative feminist author and columnist, and, via email, stay in close touch with them.

But I relished Harold Kaufman's original thinking and independence of mind, and Susan's special tolerance for Harold, a splendid jazz pianist and wonderful sparring partner over ideas of all sorts. Harold could always be counted on for a forceful point of view. Before Harold passed on to jazz player's and golfer's heaven, our last big to-and-fro was over Tiger Woods: Harold firmly disputed Tiger's every word in the golfer's statements of contrition.

Karen and I have continued to treasure Susan's friendship down to this very minute, even as another physician—also a very distinguished psychiatrist—became her new beau. He is a charming guy who obviously has good taste in women! Susan, for decades now, an authority on communications technology—particularly in the use of satellites—travels the globe to conferences and to consult for numerous clients in this field.

In my own life as a writer and publicist, I have been especially careful about which clients I even consider. A good tool comes from the philosophy of the great Tony Schwartz, famous as the producer in 1964 of the "Daisy" television ad, which depicted LBJ as a nuclear warmonger.

Sometime before Tony's 2008 death, Tom Weinberg—a writer and journalistic original who is an old and most trusted colleague of mine—interviewed Schwartz. Tom, with his videographers and Media Burn Collective, was among the earliest users of portable electronic gear for getting behind the scenes of events that would otherwise only be covered, when possible, by traditional media using cumbersome equipment.

But in Tom's interview, Schwartz expressed thoughts worth repeating:

"I've done about 450 political campaigns and thousands of commercial jobs, so

- I CHOOSE work I like, particularly the people.
- I want candidates who will do no harm.
- In politics as in everything, there are honest people and those who are not: I want to work for honest people.
- I want clients who have people around them who know what they are doing.
- I want a client that pays their bills.
- In politics like in everything, I do not work for people who "shakedown."
- I understand and approve of "negative ads."

Among Tony's books are *Media, The Second God*, and *The Responsive Chord*. This latter volume had an outsized influence on me, as Tony wrote that electronic media went directly to a recipient's brain, inevitably striking a responsive chord there. Linear, or print, media requires more thoughtful comprehension, according to Schwartz.

Another vital issue, which many journalists and novelists confront, is "writer's block." When Clay Felker was the highly praised, innovative editor of *New York* magazine, one of his staffers came to him saying he just couldn't get started. Famously, Felker told the writer, Tom Wolfe, "just write me a memo." That advice worked out brilliantly, as Wolfe invented what was called "The New Journalism," mixing fact and fiction. He went on to write many impactful books, such as *The Electric Kool-Aid Acid Test* (1968), *The* New Journalism (1975), *The Painted Word* (1975), *The Right Stuff* (1979), *In Our Time* (1980), *From Bauhaus to Our House* (1981) and *The Purple Decades* (1982).

But these days, big questions in politics and media are certainly there for anyone who chooses to take some time for these weighty endeavors. Addressing them is easier and quicker with Google around, and access to the great universities and local libraries is helpful. But sometimes instant answers can be very misleading. One of our best graduate school instructors, teaching a course in foreign policy reporting, exhorted, "Never merely trust the opinion of the first taxi driver who comes your way in an international capital."

These days, reporting on San Diego's very robust classical music scene, I'm finally getting some of the education I missed while growing up. In this reporting I am reminded of the expression of the Nobel Prize laureate, Steven Weinberg, who said that if he wanted to know about something, he would either teach a course or write a book. I guess I've adopted a journalistic version of that, reporting on something or trying to get some thoughts together on numerous topics of interest.

For instance, I was intrigued when Michael Dukakis, the former Massachusetts governor, laid out one idea on how to get maximum voter turnout. Dukakis, who lost the 1988 presidential election to George H.W. Bush, suggested that there should be 250,000 precinct captains, one for each voting location nationwide. Variants of this strategy and tactic are on the table in both the Republican and Democratic camps, but new forms of social media that might serve a similar purpose (to work directly with voters) may now supersede Dukakis' idea.

Prior to the 1988 election, I was delighted to support my longtime collaborator, the creative attorney, Steve Saferin, in putting on a debate in Houston involving most of the Democratic candidates. For this venture we had the support of the respected Billy Goldberg, an affluent Houston lawyer. Billy was a large presence in Houston when I was growing up, and he later became prominent in Texas Democratic circles. Governor Dukakis won our debate handily, but often what may happen in primaries is not necessarily a good predictor of a final outcome.

Another media adventure, one that was terrific fun, became a wonderful success. This was a television celebration of the Texas Anniversary Sesquicentennial. The series starred the quintessential Texan, Willie Nelson. Willie voiced scripts produced by Steve and me—along with my pals, the superb Texas writers, David Horwitz and the brilliant Paul Burka.

Texas Sesquicentennial Anniversary television celebration, starring Willie Nelson

Credit: David Horwitz

David became a filmmaker extraordinaire. Paul, a fine *Texas Monthly* senior writer, had also been there with me back at Rice in 1963, when President Kennedy announced the moon program.

Saferin pulled all of us together for what became *True Tales of Texas*. I was proud of our work and we made some money on the heavily sponsored TV mini-series.

Steve went on to become a top executive at Scientific Games, the world's leading producer of lottery programs. Married to Steve, and almost always expressing sound judgment, was Linda Saferin, who had gotten her start as a creative executive in producing CDs and videocassettes during a time when the internet—with its streaming video capabilities—was just emerging. For many decades Karen and I have continued to enjoy friendships with Linda and Steve, Paul and, of course, David.

CHAPTER 18

A BULLY'S PULPIT

Abrilliant political scientist, a friend, Michael Jay Robinson, who in an earlier era made an important contribution to the study of comparative media in his book, *Over the Wire and on TV: CBS and UPI in Campaign '80*, once told me, only half-jokingly, "There are only two positions in American politics: the moderate position and the wrong position." I have long—since the days when I suffered through the extremist politics that characterized my parents—thought that Michael had it just right.

For me now, passing into my mid seventies, the big, ongoing and overarching issue is health and personal wellbeing. One of our journalism school professors had warned that we should be sure to protect ourselves financially for when the legs give out or when we might disagree with editors. But I still wonder about what to do when the brain turns lazy and gives out.

Of course, ours is a stressful age, made even more so by the manipulations of the incumbent president. And it cannot be forgotten that Trump's base, and his also that of his egregious Vice President Mike Pence, may add up to more than forty percent of the American electorate. Presidential elections are almost always close, with the winner often only a few thousands of votes ahead of the loser. But in 2016 the Democratic candidate, Hillary Clinton, won the national popular count by nearly three million votes which, of course, turned out to be a virtually meaningless number, as she lost in the Electoral College.

As I grew up in journalism, I could see that *The New York Times*, along with the *Associated Press*, functioned almost like a morning inter-office newsletter for hundreds of reporters and editors. When one included *The Washington Post,* those might have been about the only news outlets everybody had to start off with in the morning.

Of course, this had often resulted in a certain sameness to the national news product. This "herd journalism" has important implications for the actions of political leaders. In a way this is not so bad for, as Thomas Jefferson had written so well in 1787, "Were it left to me to decide whether we should have a government without newspapers, or newspapers without a government, I should not hesitate a moment to prefer the latter."

But even in the early days of the nation, politicians were grumbling about the press. With more than 300 papers at the time, even President George Washington complained about the frequent criticism he was receiving. Our first national leader had to be forced to run for a second term because he did not need nor want the antagonism that was unleashed upon him by the opinionated partisan press.

Those early leaders were given a taste of what has come to dominate our national discussion, with conservatives out in the nation turning to Fox News and liberals finding comfortable offerings from MSNBC. There had once been talk that a person could get a newspaper with only the content that they wanted. This has almost come to pass, and makes one yearn for old-time objective journalism. Using new media devices and techniques, especially a personal Twitter feed, politicians—especially the unspeakable incumbent president—can now send out their own edited "news" aimed at just their own supporters. As we have noted, it is common knowledge that Trump blasts out his own often venomous words to many millions. This leaves his opponents trying to catch up, particularly since the newest communications technology had given an ugly additional meaning to the phrase "bully pulpit," first used during the time of President Theodore Roosevelt. The term means that almost anything a president offers up gets news coverage.

But now the country is sharply divided. Research specialists call this *political polarization,* and it is a condition that makes everyone wonder how our leaders can get anything done. Such an environment makes a robust free press even more vital.

This was proven to be particularly true in 2016 when Trump came along, arguing for victory by developing his own extremist base. "Where is my lawyer?" Trump asked sullenly, begging for the kind of private-sector advice he had earlier gotten from that hard-charging New York City loudmouth, the evil Roy Cohn. Cohn had been counselor to the most despicable of the red scare monsters, Senator Joseph McCarthy. Trump continues to search for someone who will say anything, do anything, to convince vulnerable people that he is best to lead our country. Of course, millions need no convincing, as they believe Trump is a proper and legitimate leader.

A line-up of distorters—most famously the former Mayor of New York City, Rudy Giuliani—have been ready to work for Trump. Among the worst in this category is the professional-sounding-and-appearing attorney Trump named to head the Justice Department, US Attorney General William Barr. Bill Barr behaves like a Trump acolyte rather than the nation's top lawyer. But this set of new Trump defenders came slam up against the constitutional protocols of our country. So, a special counsel was appointed to investigate the Trump campaign's work with Russia and its strong-arm leader, Vladimir Putin. Because of his nasty nature, Trump began to call any news reporting of these developments "fake news," a disparaging term for all news that he doesn't like.

It is true that journalism depends on the integrity of reporters, writers, editors and publishers, particularly in our internet environment when just about anyone can pose as a legitimate publisher. These days, with instant digital power widely available, it is crucial that we all employ maximum diligence to avoid scammers and fakers.

This age of Trump is in high contrast to a time forty years ago when Jimmy Carter promised, "I will never lie to you," and "The American people deserve a president as decent as they are themselves."

Sometime back, I was amused watching a segment on the CBS News program *60 Minutes*, where the insightful correspondent, Andy Rooney, said he had been down to Washington to see what our officials were up to. Rooney commented, "They need watching for sure, because they are like each of us, and you know how much we each need watching!"

Trump, in particular, needs constant watching and fact-checking, particularly of the lies and distortions he yells out at horrendous partisan rallies. His questionable slogan, "Make America Great Again," had turned into cheerleading with the referencing of constant slurs—even aimed by Trump at members of Congress. The crowd sings out "Send them back," while a smug, arrogant Trump pauses to let the crowd have at it. Then, within twenty-four hours, the president tells another of his famous lies: "I didn't encourage that." This lying behavior comes naturally to Trump.

A meeting of the American Association of Political Consultants was held in early 2017 in Huntington Beach, California, and one of the featured speakers was Brad Parscale. Parscale was under the immediate direction of Trump's son-in-law and advisor Jared Kushner, and he had figured out how to use social media to help Trump gain an electoral college victory in the election of 2016. Now in 2020, this team is reaching out to voters again in social media with incendiary words and mean-spirited lies, many of which have proven mightily effective, particularly for fundraising.

And as I began to think further of my own legacy, I pondered what it means to aspire to live up to the grandiloquent phrase, a "*citizen of the nation.*" Out here in California, I am frequently asked, "Do you miss Washington?" And the answer has become, as media outlets proliferate into many hundreds, that Washington comes to us, no matter where we find ourselves located in our great country. Three big point-of-view, 24/7 cable networks and hundreds of news sites with specialists offer their own often-sharp partisanship, and show DC machinations to us out in the nation. This often makes it difficult to avoid having a national public life, even if one so desires it.

These days it is almost mandatory to read three or four papers each morning, with a focus on the outstanding news product from *The New York Times*. I well remember how, back in Austin in the 1960s, we had to scramble over to a Texaco filling station to get a single copy of Sunday's *The New York Times*. While I still get the printed versions of my local paper, the *San Diego Union-Tribune*, as well as the *Los Angeles Times*, *Wall Street Journal* and, of course, *The New York Times*, delivered to our driveway each morning, increasingly I rely on the digital versions.

Attempts by politicians to project and control their own image are not particularly new. But what is fundamentally different, now in the age of Trump, is this president's diabolical attempt to control the news so directly. For the election of 2020, he will be continually foaming and tweeting, clamoring about "the swamp in Washington," attacking members of Congress, encouraging anti-Semitism, racism and white nationalism while hoping the American electorate fails to see through the ruse.

Thus, it is crucial not to be distracted by internet hyperbole from the president and other celebrities who spew ignorant ideas such as anti-vaccine or climate change falsehoods. This is especially the case when science and scientific research is ignored and derided by the White House.

The incumbent's use of the contemporary "bully pulpit" is a long way from President Eisenhower's tentative communication beginnings, when he offered an occasional press conference. Trump rarely has a formal news conference and mainly ignores his advisors, and instead often flings out wild charges on Twitter. As we will see, by using a Twitter account of your own, you may send out factual responses to counter his screeds.

Becoming informed and using facts to inform others is critical for intelligent use of the new media. At the same time, traditional political tactics are easily available for us all to use, to be proactive. Contact the local (or even national) headquarters for your candidate or issue. There you will be encouraged to get and distribute yard signs or simply obtain bumper stickers for your vehicles. There is no need to wait around being frustrated. We will see how the relatively uncomplicated use of social media can underscore and reinforce this important work of truth-telling.

As a young journalist, when I worked in our nation's capital, I made many acquaintances. For example, we partied with a future publisher of *The New York Times*. In the 1970's, Arthur "Pinch" Sulzberger was just a young reporter in the Washington bureau. We became professional friends through an introduction by my old high school chum, Ed Weidenfeld, and his wife Shelia, both of whom had become politically connected. Young Sulzberger frequently came around to parties and was, in due course, to become the *Times* publisher. But all that was then and this is now. Those long-ago, youthful remembrances seem tame.

Soon after Trump moved into the Oval Office, the newest *Times* publisher, the thirty-seven-year-old A. G. Sulzberger, took him on. Trump's attacks evolved from his relatively playful "failing *New York Times*" to his darker and more troubling "fake news *New York Times*" or "enemy of the people." That last is a phrase, Sulzberger noted, that has "a long and disturbing history, wording that was embraced by both Hitler and Stalin to justify the persecution and execution of enemies."

In a September 23, 2019 talk at Brown University, the *Times* publisher wisely added, "The true power of a free press is an informed, engaged citizenry." Paying attention is the beginning of winning for your candidate or cause.

When I studied political science, the word *politics* was defined as "the skill of resolving conflict." In our own time, the definition of *politics*, alas, appears to be "creating conflict."

What we see pouring out now from the Oval Office are filthy, dirty manipulative expressions. However, as the great jurist Louis Brandeis said, "The way to fight bad speech is with more speech."

All knowledgeable commentators agree that the likely winner of the presidential contest in 2020 will be the ticket of candidates who turn out the largest share of their base voters, added to the greatest number of independently minded voting citizens. Other analysts will further dive into the numbers in specific states and the strategies involved in turning out the vote.

In years past, hundreds of thousands of potential leaders and voters have been pushed away, thinking they would be unable to make a difference. This mistaken belief is harmful to our values and challenging to the very basis of democracy. But the calculation becomes easier once you focus on the crucial goal of turning out voters for your candidate or cause.

Merely reaching out via email is an easy first step for any citizen and is not to be neglected. This simply means using your personal email contact list for reaching those who can vote and contribute to your candidate or cause. If your candidate is getting national attention, look for friends and contacts in other states who might have heard about the battle and be willing to support your efforts. Use email to forward links of news stories, and ask recipients to send you links that help make the case for your candidates. Also ask them to forward your messages to contacts on their address lists who might be interested. Networking with networkers can lead to a great multiplier effect.

But further use of new media requires a bit of planning, a sound strategy and commitment. Herewith I offer other secrets, none too difficult, for getting your candidate elected and for helping your causes to prevail.

Create your own website, blog, social media page or podcast where you can post links to important news about your candidate, cause or issue, along with links to their official campaign sites. This will make it easy for people to find you on social media and to invite visitors to the site to sign up for your email list.

A main part of your campaign will involve driving traffic to the candidate or cause website that will then encourage specific actions, such as contributing money or volunteering. Creating a landing page on your own website or blog is a good idea to welcome new visitors and to immediately let them know they are in the correct place to find out more about the candidate or cause. (Merely sending visitors to your homepage can be confusing because it requires them to figure out where to go next.)

It is important to sign up on social media at least to get your own Twitter, Facebook and Instagram accounts so you can follow your candidates or causes, and re-tweet or re-post any content that seems compelling, or to send out your own factual correctives to opponent inaccuracies. Also, follow the competition on these social media sites to keep an eye on their positioning and how they might be attacking your candidate or cause.

You must know the rules of any social media platform you are using, but it is relatively easy to set up your accounts. For example, Facebook has strict rules on political speech, but there are a variety of ways to set up pages or groups in support of candidates, or to post on pages of like-minded supporters. Likewise, actively posting new material and following those with similar views is a way to gather your own followers on Twitter and Instagram. If you see fakery about your candidate, say something quickly on the same outlet to dispute the falsehoods. This includes sending letters to the editor of the newspaper to correct inaccuracies, going online to comment on a network news or cable website, and sharing these views in social media posts with your own circle of followers.

Thus, create multiple ways where it is relatively simple for supporters to take action by being informed. The goals are to increase turnout of voters for your candidate or cause, and to help them raise money to finance the campaign. Of course, you will focus on the issues and the candidates likely to support your values.

A key part of your campaign will be to find and to use influencers, that is, trusted authoritative voices, to support your efforts. Social media influencers are people who have built up large and loyal social followings, or even those who have smaller local followings. You should build a list of people who will help spread the word about your candidate. The support of even one influencer can help you reach thousands or tens of thousands of new contacts.

Make yourself available to the campaign—volunteer to hold fundraisers and host house parties, or even rallies, where the candidate or a surrogate can speak. Or, requiring less effort from you, just participate in these kinds of events. It is important, and not difficult, to notify your local TV/radio outlets and traditional print and digital news sources so they know about these gatherings. Get, or take, lots of pictures and post these on your site and on social media with hashtags that will get attention of supporters. You may be invited to be interviewed by local newspapers or on local radio and television, or to offer a spokesperson. The idea here is to show momentum.

Reach out to your campaigns to see what tools they are offering to empower other volunteers. Short texts to your peers, and other social media and canvassing tools, will be megaphones for your voice. Helping get probable supporters registered to vote, and then volunteering to drive voters to the polls, are important ways to get those less committed to cast their ballots. Watch and listen to a range of media sources to get a better idea about how your candidate is being portrayed by the competition. This will arm you with more talking points when you post your opinions.

Check in with the candidate or cause website to see what apps they are using to engage volunteers both in the field and virtually. Hopefully this is a place where you can find position papers, photos and new content to feed to your readers, viewers and followers.

Until now, only well-funded, skillful candidates have had the sophistication to generate turnout and attract voters using advanced media strategies, but now the system makes mounting a viral media campaign relatively easy and cost-effective. In this social media age, each of us now has an opportunity to energize our own tactics for engaging like-minded voters and getting them to the polls.

One's own expression can be a multiplier, clearing a path to victory, which still, of course, requires maximum voting by supporters. In the past what may have seemed an overwhelming challenge now becomes a relatively risk-free strategy of observing and acting on what you see, using your own now-powerful new media. These amazing tools make it much easier to speak out and speak up, to promote your candidate, to support your issues and to oppose those who spread falsehoods.

Taking away mob rule by a few bad actors will be easier than it seems. At first, not each of us will generate millions of Twitter followers, nor find hundreds of thousands who gladly receive emails. But it is in the aggregation of new media recipients, developed by each of us, that might best drive a return to responsible values and policies. So, don't hesitate to ask experienced social media friends and family about effective tools they are employing.

If any of this seems too complicated, or too time-consuming, or just not of interest to you, be sure to make a personal commitment using email or by getting a bumper sticker or making even a small donation to causes and candidates you support.

Promoting winning efforts to support a candidate, or a cause, is the key to unlocking the chambers of our public life.

Savvy voters in 2020 will look for honesty, authenticity and civility.

My own journeys and adventures in media have always aimed to promote these goals.

EPILOGUE

One major stimulus for me in the writing of these adventures has been a library of books and a collection of ideas. From the earliest times when we began to seek contemporary role models, a few writers have stood out, bringing perspective. Each of us reaches back to our roots to find help for our human condition. The classic writers from the religious traditions have often been a starting point.

One example of the importance and influence of ideas comes from former Vice President Al Gore. When running for president, Gore told an interviewer that the book most meaningful to him was *The Structure of Scientific Revolution* by Thomas S. Kuhn. Gore said it was not only the book, but also because he had read Kuhn's important work just as he was coming of intellectual age. Gore explained that the book carried the fundamental idea that it was the scientific method that could lead one to deeper truths.

In my own coming of age, I have especially been influenced by three contemporary memoirists: Eli N. Evans, whose *The Provincials* is the unsurpassed chronicle of Jewish life in the South; *North Toward Home*, Willie Morris' memoir of growing up in Mississippi and Texas as prelude to his Manhattan intellectual life; and *Starts and Finishes*,

Carey Winfrey's coming-of-age story about a young man's survival during the frozen frames of the Age of Kennedy.

As one of the three top students in my Columbia journalism class of 1967, Carey was awarded a Pulitzer Traveling Fellowship which he took to Hong Kong, where he worked for a local television station and freelanced for the *Far Eastern Economic Review*. Carey had been a US Marine before returning to Columbia for graduate school. Earlier, as a Columbia undergraduate, he studied English literature with some of the nation's most esteemed professors. After his return from Hong Kong, Winfrey was hired as a reporter —later a writer— for *Time* magazine where he covered media and the press. After five years as a public television producer, he became a reporter—later a foreign correspondent in Africa—for *The New York Times*. Winfrey spent the last quarter-century of his career as editor of a succession of magazines, including ten years at the helm of *Smithsonian*, before retiring in 2011.

Not long ago, Carey and I were chatting about politics and journalism, as we have done over the years. He offered an observation I thought worth pondering, one that has been off and on my mind ever since. He suggested that success in most fields, particularly for those in leadership positions, requires building a constituency of approbation and respect. As an example, Carey mentioned a former secretary of the Smithsonian Institution, the highest officer, who had been forced to resign during Winfrey's tenure as editor of their prestigious magazine. "No one much liked this guy," Carey said, "and when he cut some fairly innocuous expense account corners, they used that to get rid of him. But the real reason he was dismissed was because he had no constituency."

Similarly, when *Times* reporter Jason Blair was discovered to have made up large swathes of reporting in several stories for his paper, Howell Raines, his executive editor, was forced to resign. "Howell was quite a good editor, but he was perceived as arrogant and was widely disliked." Carey felt certain that someone with greater staff support would have survived that scandal. In other words, even at the higher reaches of professions, one should never forget the politics. I thought Carey was exactly right.

Willie Morris was something of an icon and role model for our coterie at UT. He had come out of Yazoo City, Mississippi, bringing along style and grace. We first knew Willie as the crusading editor of *The Daily Texan*, then we avidly read and were inspired by his powerful mid-life memoir, *North Toward Home*, in which Morris recalled growing up in the South before he moved on to New York to become editor of *Harper's Magazine*.

As we were all living through those years of tumultuous change, his book was particularly helpful with its focus on desegregation and the rise of LBJ. Morris's story was personal to many of us, as the volume was published just as we, too, were coming of intellectual maturity. I remember thinking that I had to get up to New York City as soon as possible!

The Provincials, the classic portrait of Jews in the South, has been re-issued almost annually since it was first released in 1973. When I first read Eli Evans's book, it often seemed to me to be my very own story. Evans had grown up as one of two sons in a North Carolina Jewish civil rights family. Their father, Mutt Evans, was the highly respected and reconciling mayor of Durham, North Carolina during the early age of civil rights improvements in the 1950s. Eli's older brother Bob, once an assistant to Edward R. Murrow, has lectured across the nation.

The Provincials explores contributions by Jews from all over the South, with an emphasis on the experience of growing up in the region. Eli says he found a unique Southern Jewish Consciousness.

Unquestionably the historian of Jews in the South, Eli is also president *emeritus* of the Charles H. Revson Foundation in New York City and a proud graduate of the University of North Carolina, as well as of Yale Law School. Evans served as a speechwriter on the White House staff of President Johnson. But, for me, Eli, with his insights—

regardless of his other impressive credentials, including being the author of several later volumes of history and recollection—has always been an important influence.

Subsequently Eli, and his delightful wife Judith, became close friends with Karen and me. Of course, Judith too, was from the Jewish South. We were amused when Eli, in New York City, got some North Carolina soil to place under the cradle of their newborn son, Josh. Decades ago on a memorable vacation trip we all took (including the baby) to Jamaica, I dreamed out loud that the little boy would grow up to be a Broadway star. As it has turned out, Josh Evans has improved on that, going national on TV as the voice behind many memorable characters.

I've gifted all my nieces and their spouses, and even members of Karen's Yankee Baltimore family, with *The Provincials* and its wonderful stories.

The impact of books came to me and many of my classmates at the University of Texas when we were exposed to "Basic Books in American History," a way of approaching the topic not merely from dry lectures but by weekly readings under the tutelage of Historian Paul Boller, with his own broad intellectual perspective. We started with a classical foundation and, over the course of a year in the 1960s, learned about the history of our country as interpreted by leading scholars. Boller has studied the American presidency and campaigns, writing several books on the topic. It has been a thrill for me to be quoted several times, and remembered in print, by this former college professor.

I also remembered practically devouring *The Uprooted* by the previously mentioned Harvard historian Oscar Handlin. What revelations were to be found there for a son of immigrants! I knew about my predecessor relatives—mostly all immigrants—but, until Handlin put their experiences into a much larger context, they could have occasionally been mistakenly seen as a bit of embarrassment. After all, as we have seen, my parents had come to the United States as children—speaking no English—and I would later sometimes think of them and some other kin as outside the mainstream. Handlin, the great Harvard historian, provided welcome context.

Fifty years later, as the Cold War was winding down, Karen and I, with support from Houston family members, brought many of Uncle Louis' progeny, including his granddaughters Elena and Svetlana, from the Soviet Union as immigrants to the United States. Here, they have achieved success as computer experts and digital designers or worked in real estate. Of particular note, Vladimir Vinogradsky started up a computer company which he sold to Microsoft, thus becoming an executive there in the bargain. His spouse, my cousin Elena Dvorkina, an artist, is in constant demand as an internet graphic designer.

They have two daughters, Louis' great-granddaughters. One, Dasha, received her undergraduate degree at the University of Chicago and a graduate degree from the Tufts University School of Veterinary Medicine. With her husband, Adam, a dedicated schoolteacher, they now live and work in Washington, DC. Dasha loves her practice with animals, and Adam works with young kids. Another great-granddaughter of Jacob, Anya Vindogradsky, is a brilliant student at California Institute of Technology, who has unlimited career potential. Svetlana and her husband Joel have also raised a successful family. Of the older family members we helped bring to the United States, some have worked and are already peacefully retired here in their adopted home country.

For my part, as a tiny boy in Youngstown, I was lucky that my father started up a grocery store in an upper-income neighborhood, while my mom began her medical practice in downtown Youngstown.

This was fine until they had to move to the Sunbelt. The story is told that Daddy had a bad sinus condition, so they gave up everything and moved to Phoenix in 1948 when I was four. I always suspected the strange relocation came because of fears that the FBI wanted my dad for his leftish politics. I have discussed my own fears, suspicions engendered when, at age eight, I found "What to do if called to testify before the House Un-American Activities Committee," a document hidden in my parents' private dresser drawers. That was a stunner, sending fear through my system, and is some of what I have described as what formed me!

Of course, the political views of my parents, as I have written, were not nearly as important as the unconditional love they bestowed on their children.

As this volume was going to press our whole world was deeply affected by the Coronavirus pandemic causing, pain, suffering, and dislocation.

Some writers, talkers and speechmakers keep going, even when they have nothing useful left to express, so permit me to use journalism's time-honored symbol (30), meaning the end.

--30--

ASK PRESIDENT CARTER

MARCH 5, 1977

A CBS NEWS CONVERSATION

For the record, the transcript, as recorded by CBS News, follows:

CRONKITE: Good day. President Carter and I are in the so-called Oval Office of the While House. We're in a couple of wing-back chairs in front of a coffee table. And in front of the fireplace across from us is the desk at which the President spends much of his day working; over to the left the large doors opening out onto the beautiful Rose Garden of the White House on a very nice spring-like day here in Washington.

This is a unique occasion, and in the sense that it marks a new approach to communication between the President and the people of the United States, it is indeed historic. Unique, historic, and we must also say an experiment, since a President has never taken part before in this sort of a broadcast.

Now here's the way we want it to work, we hope it works. We'll receive phone calls from all over the country. We expect people to ask questions on many, many subjects, of course. There'll be no censorship at all, no prescreening in that sense. However, you should know that it's not going to be easy, of course, to get through to him because there have to be just a limited number of lines coming to us here at the White House.

Now my advice is that if you get a busy signal you do like you do when you get a busy signal any time—you just hang up and try again. Now, when you do get through we'll verify your call by name and hometown. And then I'll introduce you to the president and you may talk directly with him.

Please remember that we want to give just as many of you callers as possible an opportunity to ask President Carter your questions; therefore I'm going to be just a little bit ruthless here in cutting off any long-winded statements from our callers. We do want to hear from you, the President wants your opinions and so forth, but don't make a speech, will you? In other words, get to your question right away, ask it just as clearly and directly as possible. And just as in Presidential news conferences, you will have an opportunity for a follow-up question if you think that it's necessary.

Mr. President, we're very pleased that you've accepted our CBS News invitation and are giving this time to let the nation "Ask President Carter."

MR. CARTER. Thank you, Walter. I'm glad to have a chance to let people have direct access to me. And in the process of answering 50 to 100 questions this afternoon—in an unrehearsed way, not knowing what's going to come next—I think the people will learn something and I know I'll learn a lot about what is of interest to them.

Also, I believe that if there are tens of thousands of folks who want to get through and can't do it, in listening to the other questions that are asked they're very likely to get an answer to their question. So, I'm looking forward to the two hours and whenever you're ready, I am.

CALLER NO. 1

MODERATOR. All right, Mr. President, we're ready here and I think that Joseph Willman of Sterling Heights, Michigan, is ready out there in Sterling Heights with the first question.

Q. First of all, I'd like to say good afternoon to President Carter and Mr. Cronkite. Now my question right now is, according to the U.P.I. story in today's *Detroit News*, Idi Amin has said that now he has killed 7,000 Christians. With this and other happenings there, how can we with good conscience trust a man with such an ego, and if the time arises will use force to get them out, even though a confrontation with this country is expected by Amin?

A. Well, it's hard to know how to answer that question about future events. As you know, we had what was on the border of a crisis last weekend. The attitude that we took was constantly to monitor what is going on in Uganda—to deal directly with Amin in a very forceful way to let him know that we were expecting American lives to be protected.

We also got the help of several national leaders who are quite close to Amin, primarily those of the Moslem faith, and they contacted him directly. We also got the Federal Republic of Germany, West Germany, who has diplomatic leaders in Uganda—Entebbe, Uganda—to contact Amin. And he was constantly giving me assurance through cables that the Americans would not be hurt.

As you know, the outcome of that weekend's tension was that he eventually said that the meeting with the Americans was called off and that anyone who wanted to leave or come into Uganda from out of the country would be permitted to do so.

I think that it's obvious that we'll do whatever we can to protect American lives throughout the world. We have in the past, before I became President, informed the American people in Uganda—and I might say in several other countries around the world—that there was a potentially dangerous circumstance for them. And that if they were primarily concerned with a peaceful life, they ought to change countries.

We do know that most of the persons who are Americans in Uganda are missionaries, deeply committed to their own religious faith. They've had an option to leave and they've decided to stay.

So, I think at this time I feel that the American lives there will be protected. We did act, I think, forcefully and effectively with Amin. We had a lot of help from other nations. And I can't say what I will do in the future except to try to handle the situation similarly to what I did last weekend.

CALLER NO. 2

MODERATOR: Let's take our next caller. it's Pete Belloni of Denver, Colorado.

CARTER. Go ahead Mr. Belloni.

Q. Good afternoon, Mr. President.

A. Good afternoon.

Q. Mr. President, your proposal of increasing the gasoline tax by 25 cents a gallon: would that put quite a burden on the people of this country who are already financially strapped with higher taxes and fuel bills?

A. Well, Mr. Belloni, I've never proposed any such thing and don't know where the story originated.

Q. It was in the paper last week, in the *Rocky Mountain News*.

A. I don't believe the story was attributed to me in any way because I've never commented on that at all and have never even insinuated to anyone that I was going to raise the gasoline tax by 25 cents.

Q. Have you heard about it though?

A. I had one news question about it and responded the same way I am to you—that I don't know anything about the proposal and have no intention of doing it.

I might say that on April 20, I will, if plans go the way we have them now, make a speech to the joint session of the Congress, probably in the evening, and explain for the first time in our country what a comprehensive energy policy is. We don't have one at this moment and we've been working on it ever since even before I became president.

So, April 20 we will try to spell out an approach to the energy problem that will involve all aspects of it—oil, coal, solar energy, obviously nuclear power, hydroelectric, pricing, mandatory efficiency, conservation—voluntary—and so forth. And this may or may not involve any changes in the price structure, but I certainly have not considered and have no intention of any such increases you've talked about this afternoon.

Q. Yes sir, Mr. President. Whoever brought out the story, do they know who did it or anything, or how it leaked out or anything?

A. Pete, it didn't leak anywhere from the White House because that's not a decision that's been made in the White House.

Q. I see. Well, thank you very much, Mr. President. It's been an honor.

A. Thank you, Pete, I've enjoyed talking to you.

Q. Thank you very much.

CALLER NO. 3

MODERATOR: Thank you, Mr. Belloni. The next question, Mr. President, is from Mark Fendrick of Brooklyn, New York. Mr. Fendrick, go ahead.

Q. Good afternoon, Mr. President. What I'd like to ask is in relationship to the attempts for returning to a normal relationship with Cuba. Now, in the paper the last couple of days here in New York, there's been talk about the Yankees baseball team going to Cuba. Do you think that this is a possibility in the near future, and do you think that normal relations to Cuba are possible again in the near future?

A. Well, there are varying degrees of relations with Cuba. As you know, we have had some discussions with them in the past, for instance, on the antihijacking agreement, which expires this spring. And we now have no visitation rights by American citizens to go to Vietnam, to North Korea, to Cuba and one or two other nations. We do have a procedure already in effect whereby a limited number of Americans can go into Cuba without using a passport because of prior agreement with the Cuban Government.

I would like to do what I can to ease tensions with Cuba—it's only 90 miles, as you know, from the Florida coast—and I don't know yet what we will do. Before any full normalization of relations can take place, though, Cuba would have to make some fairly substantial changes in their attitude.

I would like to insist, for instance, that they not interfere in the internal affairs of countries in this hemisphere and that they decrease their military involvement in Africa and that they reinforce a commitment to human rights by releasing political prisoners that have been in jail now in Cuba for 17 or 18 years, things of that kind.

But I think before we can reach that point we'll have to have discussions with them, and I do intend to see discussions initiated with Cuba quite early on re-establishing the antihijacking agreement, arriving at a fishing agreement between us and Cuba, since our 200-mile limits do overlap between Florida and Cuba. And I would not be averse in the future to seeing visitation rights permitted as well.

Q. In relationship, though, to the Yankees playing an exhibition game there, I've noticed that Secretary Vance has backed this idea. Do you think that that's a possibility this season?

A. It's a possibility, yes.

Q. Thank you, Mr. President.

MODERATOR. Mr. President, may I ask—it seemed that Secretary Vance indicated just the last day or so that there would be no preconditions in discussions with Cuba, are you now saying that there will be?

A. No. The preconditions that I describe would be prior to full normalization of relationships, the establishment of embassies in both our countries as they complete freedom of trade between the two countries. But you couldn't possibly arrive at a solution to some of those questions without discussions. So we will begin discussions with Cuba if they approve the idea fairly shortly, on the items that I've described—increased visitations of Americans to and from Cuba, the fishing rights question that has to be resolved for the protection of our own fishermen, and also the antihijacking agreement, which has been in effect in the past but is about to expire.

Providing Jobs for Americans
CALLER No. 4

MODERATOR: This is "Ask President Carter" on the CBS Radio Network. Now, to call the President here in the Oval Office in Washington, let us remind you of the telephone number again. It's 900-242-1611. 900-242-1611. And the next call, Mr. President, is from Miss Cheryl Clark, of Paris, Kentucky. Miss Clark.

Q. Mr. President, this is Cheryl Clark, a student at the University of Kentucky. I'd like to ask, do you consider it possible for government to create jobs similar to the W.P.A. and the C.C.C. in the Depression years in order to reduce unemployment, or do you support the Humphrey-Hawkins Bill?

A. Well, the first major proposal that I made to the Congress, which was worked out with the Congressional leaders even before I was inaugurated, was to put the American people back to work or to start that process. I think this is one of the primary responsibilities that I have as President. We've asked for a so-called stimulation package to our economy over the next two years—this one and next year—of about $31 billion, a major portion of which is either reducing people's taxes or providing direct jobs.

The jobs can be provided in a number of ways, including the one that you describe for young people, similar to the C.C.C. program we had during the Depression years back in the thirties.

In addition to that we have approved, as far as my Administration is concerned, a substantial amount of money for public works projects—that is, to build libraries, schools and other facilities in communities and that the Federal Government would have to pay for.

This work would be done by those who are employed by private contractors and the same thing would apply in the insulation of homes, in building recreation areas and employment in local and state government, perhaps, and mental institutions, health programs, teachers' aides, also in the training of primarily young people to hold a full-time job in the private sector.

And the total cost of this, as I said, is about $31 billion. And I think this is the best approach to it.

The Humphrey-Hawkins Bill is pretty much a philosophical kind of expression of our government's commitment to full employment. The Humphrey-Hawkins Bill has been constantly modified: it's never gotten out of committee either in the House or Senate. And I think some of the things that we propose this year are a substitute for some of the provisions of the Humphrey-Hawkins Bill.

I do feel, in closing, that most of the job opportunities ought to be generated permanently and in the private sector of our free enterprise system and not in Government itself. And that would be the result, I hope, of this two-year effort to stimulate an economy which is very dormant now and where the unemployment rate and inflation rate is excessively high.

Q. Okay, thank you very much.

A. Thank you, Cheryl.

Q. You'll see public confidence in Government increase.

A. Thank you.

Q. Goodbye.

<u>Family Costs In White House</u>
<u>CALLER NO. 5</u>

MODERATOR: The next call, Mr. President, is from Nick Kniska of Lanham, Maryland.

Q. Mr. President?

A. Yes.

Q. My question for you is that I would like to know why your son Chip and your daughter-in-law and grandson are living in the White House on taxpayers' money, why he is not out in his own house earning a living, O.K., instead of living off the taxpayers.

A. Well, I think you might want to know that all of the personal expenses of our family are paid for out of my own pocket or the pocket of my children. Our food is kept separate; we pay for all of it. All of our clothes and so forth are paid for out of our own pocket.

Chip is a hard-working young man and he's a great help to me. Most of my first year in office will be spent fairly close to the White House, and when we have a special problem anywhere in the nation and I want the people there to know how deeply concerned I an about it, I would like to have an opportunity to use members of my family to go and represent me personally, along with professionals who serve in the government.

I'll just give you one quick example that involves Chip directly. When we had a very serious problem in Buffalo because of excessive snowfall, I asked Chip to go up there to speak for me. He's a very knowledgeable young man and he also let the Buffalo people know that I personally cared about them. I couldn't take a full day off and go and spend a day in Buffalo, but Chip could. So, I think this is a good approach.

But I want you and the American people to know that we are not mooching off the American taxpayers. All of our family's expenses are paid for out of my own pocket.

Q. OK, this is a follow-up.

A. Sure.

Q. In the last week or so you had your grandson born in a naval hospital?

A. Yes.

Q. OK., is he entitled to special military benefits or Government benefits also?

A. No, sir.

Q. OK., then why were they in a military hospital?

A. Well, Bethesda Hospital is available for all top officials and their families.

Q. Yes. Because we're a military family, too.

A. Very good. Well, I was an old military man myself.

Q. Yes.

A. But we have health insurance and we pay the routine charges for the hospital expenses. I might say, though, in complete honesty with you, that there is a physician who is attached to the White House and who always has been. And he follows me when I go somewhere in case I get hurt or have a heart attack or something. And his services are available to the members of my family as well.

Q. OK. So in other words that's where he sent them.

A. That's correct. Now he's not an obstetrician but he is available in case I or any of my family members—or even guests in the White House—get ill during the night. He's available to take care of them and that's done at public expense.

Q. OK. thank you very much, Mr. President.

A. Sure.

Q. OK., goodbye.

A. Goodbye, Nick.

Seeking Reform in U.S. Tax Law
CALLER No. 6

MODERATOR. Mrs. Esther Thomas of Villanova, Pennsylvania, Mr. President, is on the phone. Go ahead, Mrs. Thomas.

Q. Good afternoon, Mr. President. First, I'd like to say as a mother of an American officer in the United States Army, career officer, I hope you go into history books as the first Democratic President that did not solve our nation's financial and unemployment problems by going to war. Now for my question. How can we, as middle-class earners, expect legislation or reform that would remove tax loopholes the rich or affluent use as deductions when all laws and legislation are made by the rich? There are no poor people, no lower-class wage earners in either the House or the Senate.

A. Well, Mrs. Thomas, I think you may have noticed during the campaign that I made an issue of this almost constantly and in my acceptance speech at the Democratic Convention said that I thought the income tax system of this country was a disgrace. I haven't changed my opinion about that and have initiated a comprehensive analysis of the income tax structure, and before the end of September we will propose to the American people and the Congress, in a highly publicized way, basic reforms in the income tax structure.

In the stimulation package that I mentioned earlier this afternoon, we have one provision in there that helps people like yourselves. It increases the personal exemption for a family up to $3,000, and this is a permanent change and also greatly simplifies the income tax forms, which, as you notice for 1976 calendar year that you are filling out now, are very complicated.

Q. And how.

A. Now, this average for a family, for instance, that makes $10,000 a year—this tax reduction or refund will amount to about thirty percent of the taxes paid. And the permanent reduction that will be in effect from now on will amount to about twenty percent tax reduction for that $10,000-a-year family. We anticipate in September eliminating a great number of the loopholes that do benefit the rich and the powerful, and any of those savings that are derived from that will be passed along to the low- and middle-income families like, perhaps, yourself.

Q. Thank you. And may I say as a registered Republican, I'm behind you 100 percent, and I'm sure there's a lot of us out here.

A. Thank you ma'am. I really appreciate that.

Q. Thank you. Goodbye.

MODERATOR: Mr. President, what about Mrs. Thomas's question about the Congress being loaded with the upper-middle classes and upper classes and not enough representation from the lower classes. Do you think that's true?

A. Well, I think once a Congressman gets in office now with a fairly substantial salary, they are obviously in the upper class, and so is a President, by the way. I guess so is an anchorman for CBS.

But I think that to the extent that Government officials like myself and the members of Congress make an extra effort to stay in touch with people to let folks like Mrs. Thomas ask us questions and to scrutinize who pays the bills for my family within the White House anti so forth—that's a good way to restore confidence in us.

Also, I believe that the campaigns which come every two years for the members of Congress keep them in touch with poor or working people. I know my own campaign for the last two years, joined by my wife and all my sons and their wives, my mother quite often and my sister and my aunt, we learned about people in other parts of the country outside of Georgia during the two-year period. So, the campaign process is part of our Constitutional system. I believe there's a good guarantee that to a substantial degree, public officials stay in touch with folks back home.

Now the problem is, Walter, in a case like income tax, over a period of years the laws change, and the ones who demand the changes are those who are powerful and who are influential and who can hire lobbyists or who can pay for their own private lawyer and who can form a cohesive approach to Congress and put tremendous pressure on the Congress to meet a permanent or transient temporary need. Once that need is passed, that special privilege in the law stays there.

The average American family, $10,000, $15,000 sometimes $20,000 a year, has no organization. They don't have any lobbyists, and the only way for them to understand what goes on in very complicated income tax laws is for somebody like the President to take the initiative and present to the American people in a comprehensive way, all at once, these are the things that are unfair. These are the things that can be changed to make it fair so the American people can be marshalled to exert their influence and their interest in the laws.

A person who has a special privilege, they focus their attention and their influence on that one tiny part of the law and the average American has no idea what's going on. But if I can get the whole American tax-paying body toward the end of September to join with me and demand from the Congress that we make the laws simple and fair, then in that instance I think we can overcome this deterioration, which in my opinion, has taken place ever since 1913 or whenever it was that the income tax laws went into effect. And that's why I'm so interested in having the American people not only believe that I'm acting for them but let them understand what's going on. That's the reason for this radio broadcast.

Better View of Farmers
CALLER No. 7

MODERATOR: The next caller is on the line, Mr. President. Its Mrs. Harlan Schnuhl of Brandon, Wisconsin.

Q. Good afternoon, Mr. President.

A. Good afternoon.

Q. I would like to compliment you on giving the opportunity to the American people to participate in this question-and-answer period. As a wife of a dairy farmer, my question relates to a problem concerning many such farmers.

What can be done about improving the public relations between the consuming public and the US Ag Department in regards to the price increases for farm commodities at our farm level, and the explanation to the public that we as farmers receive a small amount of these widely acclaimed increases?

A. I've got two quick suggestions: One is to put a farmer in the White House, and the other is to put an actual dirt farmer in the Department of Agriculture as the Secretary, and we've already done those two things.

Also, I think the next step is to let the American public know the truth about agriculture and the farm and ranch families of our nation. I think that the interests of consumers and the interest of the average farm family are exactly the same. I have studied the Wisconsin dairy farm industry quite at length myself during the Wisconsin primary last year. The average Wisconsin dairy family only makes about $7,000 a year, and that's with all the members of the family working on the farm—maybe three, four or more adults. There's an investment, an average investment, in the Wisconsin dairy farm of about $180,000, so if the farm is sold and the money was put in a savings account at five percent interest, the Wisconsin dairy family would have an income of $9,000 a year just from the interest, which is $2,000 more than they get from working full time on the dairy farm.

Q. Correct.

A. And if the American consumers who drink milk and eat cheese and other dairy products know for a fact that the farmers are not making excessive profits, that they work very hard seven days a week and that the return on their investment is extremely low, like three or four percent, I think they would appreciate what the farmers do, and I think a stable farm economy where the prices of milk are at least equal to production cost would guarantee that you don't have the wild fluctuations up and down in milk and wheat and cotton and beef and poultry and pork, because when the prices fluctuate wildly because the market is uncontrolled, when they go, the consumers pay the high price; the farmers have already sold their products to the middle man, and when the prices go down for the farmer, for the consumer they stay up.

So, what we are trying to do is to have a stable farm economy with predictable production as well as the weather will let us, with prices that don't fluctuate wildly and with the truth being told the consumers that what's best for them is almost always exactly what's best for the average farm or ranch family. So, I think we're making some progress in that. I might close my answer by saying that in 1977, this year, there will be a comprehensive farm bill either passed or extended from the past number of years, so we'll be addressing this on a fulltime basis, and Bob Bergland, who is a dirt farmer from the northern part of Minnesota and now the Secretary of Agriculture, I think we'll have a much better way to understand both farmers and consumers than has been done in the past.

Q. Well, thank you so much for your comments.

A. Thank you, Mrs. Schnuhl.

Dividends Tax Is Called Unfair
CALLER No. 8

Ms. Rita Karatjas, Joliet, Ill.

Q. Yes. Good afternoon, President Carter.

A. Good afternoon.

Q. I would like to know if you intend to remove the tax on savings account interest and stock dividends? I believe we're one of the only countries in the world that tax unearned income. And I feel that as income is already taxed at the payroll level, I feel it very unfair that it's taxed again after it's invested or saved.

A. Mrs. Karatjas, I can't answer that question yet. I'm not trying to avoid your question; I just don't know the answer.

Q. I see.

A. That's one of the things that we will be considering along with hundreds and hundreds of others in the comprehensive tax reform study that will be going on this year.

So I'm reluctant now to single out one particular part of the tax code and say it will not be changed, even though it might very well stay the same. I just can't answer your question now.

Q. I see.

A. I'm sorry.

Q. Thank you.

CALLER NO. 9

MODERATOR: Next questioner. Ronald Fousc, or Fouse I believe it is, of Centreville, Georgia. Mr. President. Mr. Fouse.

Q. Good afternoon, Mr. President.

A. Afternoon, Mr. Fouse. I came to Centreville the last time I was home.

Q. Yes, sir, you come through the Air Force base I work at every time you come down.

A. Very fine. Go ahead with your question.

Q. Yes, sir. Now that you've pardoned the draft evaders and you propose to pardon the junkies and deserters, do you propose to do anything for the veterans such as myself that served the country with loyalty?

A. Well, I thought I might get a friendlier question from Georgia, but I'll try to answer your question.

I don't intend to pardon any more people from the Vietnam era. I promised the American people when I was running for office that I would pardon the ones who violated the Selective Service laws; I don't have any apology to make about it and think I made the right decision.

But the deserters and others who've committed crimes against military law or civilian law will not be pardoned by me on any sort of blanket basis. My preference is to let the Defense Department handle those cases by categories or by individual cases.

We have moved, I think, already, to help—as you said—loyal and patriotic veterans like yourself. And I've appointed a very fine young man to head up the Veterans Administration now, Max Cleland, who is a veteran of the Vietnam War. This is kind of a new generation of leadership.

And within the economic package that I presented to Congress, we have a heavy emphasis on training and job opportunities for veterans. So I hope in the future that we can have a restoration in our country of appreciation for veterans who did go to the Vietnam War, who have not been thanked or appreciated enough in the past, and a much more sensitive Veterans Administration toward the Vietnam veterans who have not had as many benefits as veterans of previous wars that were more popular.

But I don't have any apology to make for what I have done, but you need not be concerned about an extension of pardons on a blanket basis in the future from me.

Q. OK., sir, thank you very much.

A. Thank you.

MODERATOR: Mr. President, there seems to be increasing talk about a bonus for Vietnam veterans. Has that been your thinking at all?

A. No, sir.

States' Rights, Women's Rights
CALLER NO. 10

MODERATOR: The next call is from Mrs. Richard Nicholson of Fort Worth, Texas, Mr. President. Mrs. Nicholson?

Q. Mr. President, 1 appreciate this opportunity to talk to you. I feel that you are violating the states' rights when you call into the different states and lobby for the ERA. I was wondering if you—don't you think that this should be left up to the individual state legislators and let them decide without interference from high political offices?

A. OK. Well, I think you probably have noticed that the final decision is with the state legislatures. And although I have made a few telephone calls since I've been in office and have talked to some personally and to some Governors about the passage of E.R.A., I haven't tried to interfere or put pressure on them.

When I ran for president I made it clear that I was in favor of the Equal Rights Amendment passing and still am in favor of it and hope it does pass. But I respect very well and very consistently the right of individual state legislators to vote the way they choose.

But I think it's good to point out to the legislators individually and to the people of the country, as I am doing at this moment, that we do need to give women equal rights. They've been cheated too long. They don't have equal pay for equal jobs and I think that this Equal Rights Amendment, which is very simple and very clear, would be a good thing for our country.

So, I don't have any way to make a legislator vote against his or her wishes. I don't want any influence on them but reserve the right to express my opinion just like you have a right to express yours.

Q. Except that I don't have the power to make or break someone that you do.

A. I don't have that power, either, Miss Nicholson.

Q. OK. Now that'd be all right. Nowhere does it mention anything about women's rights. And there is the equal pay opportunity, which is already a law, that is being used, so how can the E.R.A. help in these two areas?

A. I think the Equal Rights Amendment just simply says that the Congress nor any state are not permitted to discriminate against women. And I would presume that you would agree with that statement, but apparently you don't.

Q. Well, certainly I do.

MODERATOR: Well, thank you very much, Mrs. Nicholson.

A. Thank you, ma'am.

Q. Thank you.

Amount of Help For Taxpayers
CALLER NO. 11

MODERATOR: Thank you.

Let's do move on. We want to get as many questioners in as possible today. Mike McGrath of Warsaw, Indiana, has won the lottery to get on the air here. Mr. McGrath, go ahead with your question to President Carter.

Q. Yes, sir, Mr. President, sir. Are you there?

A. Yes, sir, go right ahead, Mike.

Q. OK. A little quotation now—I was awful proud to serve in the Vietnam War there. I was aboard that USS Constellation there, there in North Vietnam, there.

A. Yes.

Q. But at any rate, is that there tax rebate supposed to be for $50, or, or what?

A. I think it will be more than $50 for some people, depending on what your income is.

Q. Oh.

A. The ones that make above $25,000 or $30,000 a year don't get any rebate, according to the latest action of the Congress, and that means that a little bit more would be available to those at the lower levels of income.

Q. Oh.

A. In addition to that, there's a special provision for allocation of funds to veterans, like yourself, and in addition we have a tax reduction that's permanent by giving a higher personal exemption of $3,000 for a married couple—I think the latest version is $2,400 for a single person—so you get about an equivalent of a thirty percent reduction in your income taxes for 1976, if you're at the $10,000 or so level.

Q. You mean it might be a little bit lower than that?

A. Well, if you have a real high income like you seem to have, you might get a little bit lower, but it won't be much lower than 50,000, than $50 in the tax rebate unless you are well above the $25,000 level, and in addition, as I said, you'll get the permanent reduction in your income taxes brought about by the higher personal exemption. That'll stay on the books even after the stimulation package is gone.

Q. Oh, O.K.

A. It's a pretty good deal for you, I think.

Q. I think so. Now, another thing was, there's somebody told me at the factory where I work at, that Peabody, American Brands, somebody told me that the G.I. Bill is supposed to have been reactivated or something? Is there anything to that at all?

A. Mike, I don't know about the latest version of that, but if you'll listen in on the radio program for the next 10 or 15 minutes, I'll get the answer for you and give it to you in a few minutes. Okay?

Q. That's fine, O.K., that's fine. Thank you, Mr. President.

A. Thank you, Mike.

MODERATOR: I might note that the President has a plan for just that—if he doesn't have the answer here, he's got a couple of aides standing by to see if they can get them. It is

Saturday afternoon, a lot of government offices are closed, but he's going to do his best to get them for you.

A. I might say, Walter, that if I can't find the answer before we go off the air, I'll call Mike personally, Monday, and give him the answer if I can.

CALLER NO. 12

MODERATOR: Let's remind all of our listeners out there that the toll-free number to reach the President here at the White House is 900-242-1611, 900-242-1611. Now, Mr. President, we have a young man, thirteen years old, I'm told, in Ridgecrest, California, John Herold, who has a question for you. John, go ahead.

Q. Good afternoon, Mr. President.

A. Good afternoon, John. How are things in California?

Q. Fine.

A. Good deal. What's your question?

Q. Since the West is having a drought and the East has too much snow, instead of shifting the snow in boxcars to the South, why not ship it West?

A. Well, we're not shipping snow South in boxcars. I think somebody made a study of that, John, and found that it would be too expensive to try to ship snow to the West.

We are very concerned about your drought. And I know that you're—I'm not sure how far north Ridgecrest is, but I know that there's an appeal by your Governor not to waste water. And I believe that in the future, along with energy conservation, we're going to have to start worrying about water conservation.

We've had too much snow in the East. Most of it's melted already, so we don't have any snow to ship even if it wasn't very expensive. That's a good thought though, and it was investigated quite thoroughly, I think, a couple of weeks ago when Buffalo, for instance, had accumulated about four or five feet of snow.

Good luck to you, John, and thanks for calling in.

Q. Thank you.

Better Benefits Under Medicare
CALLER NO. 13

MODERATOR: The next call is from Mrs. Helen Heller of Vineland, New Jersey.

Q. Good afternoon, Mr. President.

A. Good afternoon, Mrs. Heller.

Q. Thank you for this opportunity to talk to you. My question concerns the Medicare program. Does H.E.W. have any plan to re-evaluate this program with the possibility of extending benefits to senior citizens so as to reimburse them for things like needed dental care, eyeglasses and their medications? The cost of these items are so often beyond our fixed Social Security income and yet they're vital necessities to us.

A. Yes, ma'am. those things are all under consideration. We are now in the process of reorganizing the internal structure of the Department of Health, Education and Welfare so that we can put the financing of health care under one administrator. This will help a great deal to cut down on the cost of those items for people like yourself.

Also, we are freezing the amount of money that you'd have to pay for Medicare this coming year. Although the price of health care has gone up about fifteen percent a year the last few years, we're trying to prevent your monthly payments from going up for this coming year.

Q. Yes, that's good.

A. Additionally, we have introduced into the Congress a bill that would hold down hospital costs and try to prevent health care costs from going up faster than other parts of our economy. There's been a great deal of maladministration, or poor administration, of the health cost. I hope that over a period of years—and it's not going to come easily—that we can have a comprehensive health care plan in our country.

It will be very expensive, but the first step has got to be to bring some order out of chaos in the administration of the health problems we've already got, and to help poorer people—like perhaps yourself, I don't know what your income is—be able to prevent rapidly increasing costs of programs like Medicare.

So, we are at least freezing your Medicare costs if the Congress goes along with our proposal. And over a period of years we'll try to expand the coverage of the health care services for all citizens like you.

Q. Well, thank you very much, Mr. President.

CALLER NO. 14

MODERATOR: The next caller is Miss Phyllis Dupere of Rehoboth, Massachusetts. Miss Dupere, the President's on the line.

Q. Hello, Mr. President.

A. Good afternoon, Phyllis.

Q. I'm a recent graduate from college and I majored in science and my question is about the space shuttle program. If you had the opportunity to go on one of the missions, would you go and why or why not?

MODERATOR: You're talking about a space mission, Miss Dupere?

Q. The space shuttle program.

A. Oh, I see. Miss Dupere, I'm probably too old to do that. I don't know if I could start now and train and get ready to go. When I was a younger person I was always very eager to do the most advanced and sometimes quite dangerous things. As soon as our country had the idea of having atomic power to propel submarines I was one of the first ones to volunteer and was one of the very earliest submarine officers to go into the atomic power program.

And I am thinking about in the next few weeks going with Admiral Rickover out on one of our atomic submarines to ride on that. As a President it's part of my duty to learn about things of that kind.

But I can't tell you that I'm ready to go on a space shuttle. I think I just don't have the time to get ready for it.

I might say that my sons would like very much to do it, but not me.

Q. Do you think your daughter would?

A. I think perhaps she would, yes. She's a very innovative young lady and is always trying for new things and I think she's competent to be a pilot in a space shuttle in the future or to be a member of Congress, or even to be President, yes, ma'am.

Q. O.K., thank you. Goodbye.

MODERATOR: You know, Mr. President, with that shirtsleeve environment, so-called, of the shuttle, they're holding out a little hope that some of us fellows may get a chance to go along.

A. I'm interested in that program, by the way. I think this is going to be a much cheaper means by which we can perform our very valuable flights in space and still return the costly vehicle back to earth. I'm very interested in that.

MODERATOR: It's going to mean the utilization of space. We're getting past the exploration stage, I think, now.

A. We are using it now. And I think, as you probably know, with space satellite photography we not only guarantee the security of our country, but we do a great deal of analysis of crop conditions, topographical mapping to see how far it is between places, highway planning, and this is a good way, too, by the way, from either high-flying airplanes or space, to analyze waste of energy, to see where we are not insulating adequately, etc.

And so, for all those reasons, even things that are very common, like growing crops, or mining or building highways or cutting down on heat losses, we are already using space vehicles for those purposes.

Getting Away From Pressures
CALLER NO. 15

MODERATOR: The next telephone call is from Ms. Susan Allen of Cheyenne, Wyoming, Mr. President.

Q: Yes, Mr. President?

A: Yes, Susan.

Q: O.K., my question is: When you're President, do you ever get overwhelmed with your duties and just feel like getting away from it all, and if so, do you have a place to go, you know, when you get away from your duties?

A: Well, yes, I do, Susan. I felt the same way when I was Governor, and I felt the same way when I was a candidate, and I felt the same way on occasion when I was a farmer, or when I was in the submarine program.

I might say that I've enjoyed this first six weeks of being President. I have a very good staff to help me, and the working conditions are good. My house is close to my office, and I've got a good Cabinet and so far, the American people have been very supportive. I think most people in the country want me to do a good job, and that helps me a lot.

I do have a place to get away. We have been down to Georgia on one occasion since I've been in the White House, and while down there my wife and I were able to go out in the woods and in the fields. I like to hunt arrowheads and she and I walked for hours in the open fields looking for arrowheads—just as a hobby—and we have a chance to hold hands, to talk to each other about things all alone.

Q: Yeah.

A: We've been to Camp David once. It's a beautiful place in the Catoctin Mountains about an hour and a half away from here by automobile. It's a camp that President Roosevelt used when he was President and it's available to Presidents and some of the Cabinet members as well. We've been there on one occasion. So we have a chance to get away, and I might add in closing that the White House living quarters on the second and third floor where I and my family live is quite private, and we've enjoyed living there very much.

Q: Are you in favor of solar heating?

A: Yes, I am. I think this is an area where we need to expand our research and development programs, and I think that in years to come you're going to see in my Administration, and from Presidents who come after me, a very heavy emphasis on the use of solar power.

Q: Yeah, we have a solar house.

A: Oh, do you? How does it work?

Q: It's worked pretty good so far, but Buffalo and all those places have gotten all the snow, so when we have a chance to we'll check it out in a real big blizzard, but it's been working really good,

A: Oh, very good. Thank you very much, Ms. Allen.

Army's Plans to Shut Arsenal
CALLER NO. 16
Bob Mitchell, Philadelphia, Pennsylvania

Q. Good afternoon, Mr. President.

A. Hi, Bob.

Q. How are you?

A. Fine.

Q. I'd just like to say that this is truly an honor to he speaking to you on this historical occasion. I live in Drexel Hill, Pennsylvania, but I work at the Living History Center in Philadelphia, which I'm calling you from today. While visiting Philadelphia just before Election Day, Mr. Mondale pledged to keep the Frankford Arsenal open. The arsenal employs many people in this area and is an important part of our defense system. How can you justify the Army's insistence on closing down this institution, which is both a national necessity and a necessity to this area, which is already overburdened by the economic depression?

A. Bob, I might say that if there's one question that the Vice President has talked to me more about than any other thing since I've been in the White House, it's been the Frankford Arsenal. And he and I have a deep personal interest in the Frankford Arsenal.

Under the previous administration, the decision had already been made final to close down Frankford. And we are reassessing the possibility of keeping it open, at least in some form.

If it is a final decision by the Defense Department that the arsenal be closed, I'll do everything I can to honor the

Vice President's commitment and to try to orient some other kind of Federal project into the Frankford Arsenal area, so that the people will not suffer any more than necessary economically.

But we're doing the best we can on that. The closing-down had gone so far when I became President, it's almost impossible to reverse it. But we are aware of your problem, and we'll just have to do what I think's best for the country and at the same time try to honor the promise that the Vice President made to do the best he can to keep it open.

Q. O.K. Well, thank you, Mr. President.

A. Thank you, Bob.

Q. Right, bye.

Way of Curbing Narcotics Abuse
CALLER NO. 17

MODERATOR: Mrs. Phyllis Rogers of Albuquerque, New Mexico is on the phone, Mr. President. Mrs. Rogers.

Q. Good afternoon, President Carter.

A. Good afternoon, Mrs. Rogers.

Q. Thank you again for the invitation to the Inauguration.

A. Did you come?

Q. Two questions. Would it be possible to eliminate the word drugs from drug store advertising? Also, when new drugs are invented, they always use the word "drug." Why not use the terminology "medication"? Maybe it would discourage drug abuses.

A. I think that's a good idea. I was talking yesterday, just coincidentally, Mrs. Rogers, to Dr. Peter Bourne, who is now the head of my entire drug control effort, and he will be working with foreign countries, including your neighbor of Mexico, and with the Congress and others, to try to hold down the abuse of drugs. As you know, this applies not only to the illegal drugs like heroin and cocaine and marijuana and others, but it also applies to some of the medications that you've described. The barbiturates, for instance.

There is a developing question about whether they are necessary at all, and Dr. Bourne pointed out to me that the No. 1 drug that causes death is heroin, and the second is barbiturates, which is a medication that's used quite frequently by medical doctors. So the two are mixed in the people's minds and I think that "medication," as you suggested, is a better word.

I'm not sure if you could name the dispensers of that, though, medication stores. They might object to that. Maybe there's a better word. Maybe "pharmacy" would be best. But I don't have any authority over what they name it, but that's a good idea—to separate the two, the illegal drugs from the legal medications, would be a good distinction.

Q. Thank you. And the other question is: We are very concerned about the solar energy program here in the State of New Mexico, and we're hoping it will go through for us. Can you comment?

A. I don't know what the decision will be. I don't intend to get involved in the decision personally. I would like to see the research and development programs for solar energy be decided on a merit basis and where the installations are best. I would say, though, that New Mexico has a head start on many of the places around the country because of the long history of research and development and because of your climate. But I think we'll have several places around the country. But we will be doing an increasing amount of research and development on solar energy in the future.

Q. We love you, President Carter, and thank you very much.

A. Thank you very, very much yourself. I've just gotten an answer, by the way, that I'd like to give as well as I can to Mike McGrath from Warsaw, Indiana, regarding the G.I. Bill.

President Ford had recommended terminated benefits under the G.I. Bill for all persons who entered military service after January 1, 1977. He wanted to cut the period of eligibility for veterans who had entered military service before this time from 10 years to eight years. During the campaign, I came out against these actions and supported strengthening of the G.I. Bill and to hold to the 10-year period of eligibility. In the budget that I just put into place, the 10-year period will remain for Vietnam veterans for the G.I. Bill. So that answer, I think, is a good one for Mike, and I hope that he's still on the air to listen to it.

Appeal to End Ban on Laetrile
CALLER NO. 18

MODERATOR: We'll remind you that to reach the President here in the Oval Office of the White House, the number to call is 900-242-1611. In some areas there is an access code for long distance. If there is, you use it and then you dial 900-242-1611. And having successfully done that, Mrs. Opal Dehart of Trinity, North Carolina.

A. Good afternoon, Miss Dehart.

Q. Good afternoon, President Carter, I'm happy to have the opportunity to speak with you.

A. Well, it's nice to talk to folks from North Carolina. You got a question for me?

Q. Well. I really have more of a statement to make and a request.

A. O.K.

Q. My father has terminal cancer. He found out a month ago. He's a hardworking man all his life and never made much money and doesn't have much now. And for several years I've been reading about Vitamin B17, Laetrile.

And I feel that the people in this country should be permitted to use this treatment in this country. I realize that the A.M.A. says it's not been proved safe, but for a terminal patient who is not going to live—and has a chance to live with it—I don't see how it could be dangerous.

And hospital insurance does not cover treatment not authorized by the A.M.A. And most hard-working people in this country cannot afford treatments if not made under insurance benefits.

And if a person has money available to leave the country for treatment in one of the 17 countries where cancer specialists use this successfully, they have a chance of recovery. And a lot of people even from my area have done this.

What I want to say is that we need your help, and the government's help, in checking this vitamin out so that it's made available to the American people.

A. All right, Mrs. Dehart. I might let someone from the Department of H.E.W. give you a call Monday and talk to about it further. You didn't ask me a question, but I've heard about the controversy. I know that in some of our neighboring countries—I think Mexico—you can buy the Laetrile and be treated with it.

Q. That's right.

A. Why don't you let me have someone call you Monday, if you don't mind. It wouldn't help much if I called you because I don't know—I'm not a medical doctor, I'm not familiar with it. Would that suit you O.K.?

Q. Yes, sir, it would. I just wanted you to be aware and maybe that something could be done. There's an investigation needed. I know that right now it's mainly because of the 1953 ban in the State of California, and that's a little outdated and has not been tested. And the doctors who signed the papers at that time had not tested it. They went on somebody else's word.

MODERATOR: Well, thank you Mrs. Dehart. I know the President is going to have you called on that. It is a matter that concerns a lot of people in the United States.

MR. CARTER. Yes. Walter, I might say that one of the things that concerned the medical profession in permitting the use of a drug that might not be harmful—and may not do any good, either one—is that it sometimes causes people not to seek treatment because they're depending on a worthless drug.

I'm not trying to make a judgment on this one, but I know that that's a concern to us.

CALLER NO. 19

MODERATOR: Mr. O. B. Parris of Vinemont, Alabama, on the phone, Mr. President. Mr. Parris?

Q. Yes, Mr. President. I'm Red Parris with Gulf Oil, I'm a jobber for Gulf Oil Company, here in Cullman, Alabama, also Goodlet Construction Company, and I was wondering how you feel on the vertical divestiture of the oil companies, vertical and horizontal divestiture of the oil companies.

A. The position that I took during the campaign, Mr. Parris, is the same one that I have now. I think as a general proposition, vertical integration of major industries is nothing, is not contrary to the best interests of American people, provided you have a continued and adequate competition.

I am concerned on two ends of the vertical integration process. One is that there be an ensured competition for leasing rights. I think it would be a mistake for us though to require a different company to drill for oil, to extract the oil from the ground, to pump the oil to a refinery, to do the refining, and then to distribute it and then to wholesale it and then to retail it. If different companies had to do all those processes, I think that the price of the final product, like gasoline, would be greatly increased, because of inefficiency.

Q. That is true.

A. I think at the wholesale and retail level, there have been occasions that I have witnessed when there has been an inadequate amount of competition, and sometimes the small and independent service station operators have been forced to shift toward the majors, and this particularly did occur in the initial stages of the 1973 embargo period.

I have a concern also about horizontal investments when the major oil companies acquire over a period of time a controlling interest in, say, coal mining operations. It means, quite often, that there is not a heavy enough emphasis placed on increasing coal production.

So, at the wholesale and retail level, I have some concern, and in the horizontal investment by oil companies like in coal or uranium, I have some concern, unless I'm convinced that there's adequate competition there. I would be in favor of considering divestiture, but my first preference would be to ensure competition through the antitrust laws and disclosure of profits at the individual levels of the vertical integration rather than divestiture itself.

Q. Yes, sir. Thank you very much.

A. Thank you, Mr. Parris.

Finding Controls For Coffee Price
CALLER NO. 20

MODERATOR: The next caller is Mr. Dale Butkovitz of Peru, Illinois. Mr. Butkovitz.

Q. Yes, good afternoon, Mr. President.

A. Good afternoon, Dale.

Q. Yes, I have a question here. This relates with this recent coffee situation. My question is: Can we see any prospect of lower imported commodities on such as coffee, and if so, how can we go about it?

A. Is your name pronounced But-ko'vitz or But'-kovitz?

Q. But-ko'-vitz.

A. I don't know how to answer your question about the future. As you know, the Brazilians and other coffee producing countries claim that the drought—or freeze, I think it was—destroyed a number of the coffee trees and that's the reason for the high prices. I think there are adequate reserves on hand now, but the future crops of coffee are likely to be very short and the prospect of short seasons have forced up the price.

I don't know how to deal with this. There's no way for us to control the price of coffee that comes in—from Colombia, or Brazil or Costa Rica to our country—to our own nation. I think that we have one opportunity, as consumers, and that is to drink less coffee as the price goes up. This is almost inevitable in a free-enterprise system.

I'm here for two hours without moving and, just coincidentally, I'm drinking hot tea now instead of coffee. I don't want us to put an embargo on coffee use, but I don't know how to answer your question any better than that. I don't know what the future holds. I don't think that we can do anything to control the price of coffee except to reduce consumption.

Q. Mr. President?

A. Yes, Dale.

Q. God bless you and I wish you all continued success. You're doing a fine job.

A. Thank you very much, Dale, that was nice of you.

Disabled Oppose A Tax Revision
CALLER NO. 21

MODERATOR: Now let's take another call. It's from Mr. Phillip Roche, Tooele, Utah. Mr. Phillip Roche Tooele of—or Mr. Phillip Roche of Tooele, Utah. Let's go through it once more, Mr. President. We might as well spend the afternoon with this: Mr. Phillip Roche of Tooele, Utah.

Q. That's Too-ella.

MODERATOR: All right. Thank you, sir. It is Ro-shay', though, is it?

Q. It is Ro-shay,' yes sir.

MODERATOR: I got that much right.

A. Phillip, go ahead with your question.

Q. Mr. President, are you familiar with the sick leave portion of the 1976 income tax revision?

A. What was the first part of the—I heard the 1976 income tax revision—what's the first part?

Q. The sick leave portion of the 1976 income tax revision.

A. Yes, I'm fairly familiar with it.

Q. Well, my question is this, Mr. President: Are those that can't qualify for their Federal medical retirement now, could they possibly be given their jobs back?

A. I don't know.

Q. The 1976 income tax revision changed the agreement to which these people retired at, and by changing the agreements, people making $300 and $400 a month are going to have to come up with four, five, six hundred dollars for their 1976 income tax due to a clause in that sick leave portion.

A. Mr. Roche, perhaps Walter could answer that question. I don't know, but I'll have my staff see if I can get the answers, and if I can't give it to you on this program, I'll give you a call Monday and try to answer your question.

Q. (Mrs. Roche) That would be great. But Mr. President.

A. Yes, ma'am.

Q. We were allowed formerly—the truly disabled ones were allowed, you know—up to $100 a week tax deduction if they were truly disabled. Well, even though they're truly disabled now, this new revision has taken away that exclusion.

MODERATOR: Well, I tell you—I gather that's Mrs. Roche, is it?

Q. (Mr. Roche) That's the boss.

MODERATOR: Well, I tell you, the President's going to look up this question for you. It's a rather complicated one. He's going to see if he can get an answer for you and get back to you. The question's almost as difficult as pronouncing Tooele, or Tooele.

A. (Mr. Roche) Tooele.

MODERATOR: Tooele. Thank you. Thank you very much, Roches. Glad to talk to both of you.

CARTER. I'll call you back personally Monday and talk to you then. O.K?

Tax on Couples, Costly Housing
CALLER NO. 22

MODERATOR: Now Mr. Charles Stone, Mr. President, of Dallas, Texas.

Q: Two questions, sir: Having recently completed figuring the income tax for my fiancée and myself, the tax difference was $1,000 between single and married. When and what action do you plan to take? Also, in the news, you recently stated that the cost of a new home was out of reach for most Americans. Is there anything that can be done about the price or the interest rate?

A: Mr. Stone, the only thing that I know of that can cut down the price of interest rates would be to control inflation, and we have been working for the last six weeks on a comprehensive approach so that we would know in Washington, and so the American people can be informed, about all the things that we do that cause an increase in interest rates.

In addition, for low-income families, or middle-income families, we're trying to stimulate housing construction by helping with the repayment of your mortgage on a monthly basis. I hope to increase the amount of guaranteed loans for people like yourselves, and I hope this will be a lot of help to you in the years to come. We've increased the authorization for home construction by between $8 billion and $9 billion, which is an awful lot of money—of course that extends over 40 years in the future.

To answer your first question, I would like to see in a tax reform package a removal as much as possible of any sort of tax advantage for either single people or married people. This is a complicated question, and 1 don't know how to deal with it. We have now, in some parts of the income tax laws, a fairly substantial reward for people who live in the same house but who are not married, and I would like to remove that, but at the same time let people who are single and who live alone, not as married people, not be punished.

So that's one of the complicated questions that has always been a matter of debate, both in the state and national legislatures. I don't know how to give the answer yet, but there is a great disparity now.

Q. Yes, sir, you will have an answer, I believe you said, in September in your tax package.

A. I hope so. We're going to address that issue, and I hope we can come up with a reasonable answer. We're going to complete the study of this entire tax code, which is enormously complicated as you know, and the deadline that I've established and the Secretary of the Treasury, Mike Blumenthal, is the lead Cabinet officer on it, has agreed that we can complete this study and make our recommendations to the people and to the Congress by September 30. yes.

Q. Very good. Thank you, sir.

A. Good luck to you.

MODERATOR: Did I understand you to say there that you would penalize unmarrieds living together?

A. No, I just don't think there ought to be an advantage between married people and the unmarried people who share the same household. I'd like to remove, if possible, any advantage one way or the other, Walter.

CALLER NO. 23

MODERATOR: Mrs. John Ritchey is on the phone, Mr. President. She's in Georgetown, Kentucky. Mrs. Ritchey?

Q. Thank you, Walter. Good afternoon, Mr. President. I am part American Indian and am a descendant of the Ottawa tribe of northern Michigan. We presently have a bill in the Senate, Bill no. 1659. This was awarding us payment for sale of land to the Government. But the Government is once again dragging its feet, you know, for fire services and things like this. I would like to know if you're aware of this bill and if you can help us in any way. This originally started in 1870 as a signed treaty. There was a partial payment made in 1910, but since then, nothing.

A. The answer to your first question is easy. And the answer is no, I'm not familiar with the bill. The answer, if it will help you or not, I'll help to this degree. I will look into the bill and see what I think is a right and a fair thing to do. If it seems to me that the particular Indian group to which you refer has not been treated fairly, then through the Department of Interior and the Attorney General, I'll give you what help is proper. And I'll either be back in touch with you this coming week or let one of my staff members call you back and see what we think about the legislation that you have described. OK?

Q. OK This is something, you know, that we have worked on with our ancestors, you know. They've all died and, you know, this is something that they've talked about, and these are hopes and dreams that have never been fulfilled.

A. I understand. Well, I think as you probably know in Maine and Massachusetts and several places around further West and South, there's a great new analysis of whether or not

Indians have been treated fairly and legally in the past. And I would believe that I and the Congress would want to treat your ancestors or their descendants, including yourself, fairly about it; but I'll look into the bill personally and let you hear from me or my staff about it.

Q. O.K. Thank you, sir.

A. Thanks for calling.

CALLER NO. 24

MODERATOR: Next call, Mr. President, is from the Reverend James Baker in Ridgeland, South Carolina.

Q. Good afternoon, Mr. President.

A. Good afternoon.

Q. First, sir, 1 would like to commend you for the effort that you have made to restore ethics and morality in government. I think you've taken a splendid action in that direction and I wonder if more cannot be done to protect the consumer from shoddy merchandise, or warranties that are not honored, and similar unconscionable profit actions on the part of a minority in our country, either through the Federal Trade Commission or a Consumer Protection Bureau, sort of, set up.

A. If I don't do that, Reverend Baker, before I go out of office, I will consider my Administration being a failure. You are absolutely right. In many instances the regulatory agencies in Washington have been staffed and led by men and women whose primary interest is not to the consumer at all, but to the industries being regulated.

So far, we've not been able to get passed the legislation for establishing a consumer protection agency, and the consumers' interests quite often are supposed to be protected by a little tiny group of people in many dozens, even hundreds, of agencies scattered throughout the City of Washington.

So, I'm in favor of the establishment of a Consumer Protection Agency itself to focus the consumers' interest—in one agency as much as possible. This agency would be quite small. I think the budget would be in the neighborhood of $11 million a year for the entire nationwide coverage, and it would let you and I and other people know where to go to register a complaint and it would also have a group of people there whose only interest would be to protect people like you from being cheated.

So, I'm strongly in favor of that and I believe that before the next year or two goes by we'll have the new agency in operation. And I wish that you would examine every one of my appointments to these regulatory agencies that have taken place now and that will take place over the next four years, and I believe in every instance you'll see that the people that I do appoint have their obligation to the consumer. And that's the way it should have been in the past.

Q. You see, the consumer with a small complaint is not able to pay an attorney, naturally, to handle it for him. Where a consumer, you know, has a $25 or $50 complaint, he has nowhere to turn unless he has an agency that can handle it for him. Many of these are poor people.

A. You're right. I favor, in certain instances, the right—increased right—of consumers to file class action lawsuits—where a thousand consumers who have been cheated can get together and get some relief from unfair trade practices.

And also, on occasion the consumers ought to have an increased right to have legal standing in court, and I think that within the government itself quite often the consumers are not treated fairly. That's why I believe it is better to have a separate agency for consumer protection itself.

Q. Thank you. You certainly have the prayers of the American public for a successful term of office.

A. Thank you, Mr. Baker.

Cleric Dies After Talk On Phone With Carter

COLUMBIA, S. C., March 5 (AP)—A minister died of a heart attack today *shortly after* talking to President Carter on the President's call-in program.

"He talked to the President and passed away," his wife said.

The Rev. James Baker, 56, talked to President Carter about 2:15 P.M., then suffered a heart attack. He was taken to a hospital where he was pronounced dead at 4:40 P.M.

"He was very elated and delighted to have talked to the President and was looking forward to seeing it on TV," the minister's wife, Louise, said.

Mr. Baker, like the President, was a Baptist. He was pastor of the Robertville Baptist Church in Robertville.

In Washington, a White House spokesman said that President Carter and his wife, Rosalynn, had sent a telegram of condolence to the minister's family.

MODERATOR: Mr. President, when do you expect to send legislation—a proposal for legislation—to establish a consumer agency up to the Hill?

A. Well, the legislation, Walter, as you know, made a lot of progress last year and my own inclination is to support the legislation that was already considered by Congress. And I believe that with the support of the White House, instead of the opposition that was the case under the previous Administration, it'll be passed.

MODERATOR: You'll support the present legislation as it's now at the Hill, then?

A. Yes. I wouldn't want to say that I'll support in any language that's put in it, but if I can approve the basic language I'm strongly in favor of the agency, yes.

CALLER NO. 25

MODERATOR: The next caller, Mr. President, is John Melfi of Johnson City, New York.

Q. Good afternoon, Mr. President.

A. Good afternoon, John.

Q. I know we have a foreign aid policy to help countries in need, but why do we spend so much on this when we have so much poverty, unemployment and such in our own country?

A. Well, John, I'm going to take a position that's not very popular, politically speaking. We only spent about three-tenths of one percent of our gross national product on foreign aid, which is about half of the proportion that is allotted to this purpose by other countries like France and Germany and so forth. I don't particularly want to increase this greatly, but I would like for it to be predictable.

Also, in the past we've not had foreign aid used in an effective way. As one of my friends has said quite often, "I'm not in favor of taxing the poor people in our rich country and sending the money to the rich people in the poor countries." And quite often that's been done in the past.

We have also a need, in my opinion, to support the lending institutions—the International Monetary Fund, the World Bank. They give aid to other countries in the form of loans, sometimes low-interest loans. But instead of just handing gifts out that are kind of bad as a basic philosophy and also that are abused, I would favor contributing to the capital stock of these international or regional lending agencies. And I believe we'll get a lot better return on our money.

And I might say that my own experience in this first six weeks has been that the International Monetary Fund, for instance, and the World Bank are quite strict on a nation that makes a loan. They make them work hard toward balancing their budget. Quite often they require them to clean up corruption. They make them assess very carefully their trade policies.

So, I believe that the lending procedure in foreign aid is much better than the gift procedure. And when direct grants are made, we ought to do more than we have in the past to get the grants to people who actually need it.

Within those changes. I think that our present level of foreign aid is about right, John.

Q. O.K. Thank you, Mr. President. Best of luck to you in the future, and I hope you're there for another eight years.

A. Thanks very much.

I might say, Walter, that there's a Mr. Otto Flaig of Milwaukee, Wisconsin: his telephone number, unfortunately for him today, is 242-1611. And ever since 6 o'clock this morning he's been getting calls from people who want to talk to me, and he has requested me to announce that people please dial the "1" and then the "900" before they dial the 242-1611, so his phone will quit ringing.

MODERATOR: I assume those calls could only get to him from the Milwaukee area, and if they once dial the 900, it won't get through to him at all.

A. I'd like to ask people—I guess there are other folks around the country that've got the same last seven numbers, so everybody ought to remember to dial the 900 before the seven [numbers].

MODERATOR: I wonder if that gentleman in Milwaukee is giving them any answers. Maybe he's giving them quite satisfactory solutions to their problems.

A. Yes, I'm sure he's getting a lot of questions. His answers are probably better than mine.

Drafting Women for U.S. Service
CALLER NO. 26

MODERATOR: We have a call from Lapeer, Michigan, from Miss Colleen Muir. She's 16 years old, I'm told, Mr. President. Go ahead, Miss Muir.

MODERATOR. . . . Muir, I believe it is. Muir, is it, Miss—?

Q. Muir.

MODERATOR. Muir. She is 16 years old, I am told, Mr. President. Go ahead, Miss Muir.

Q. Good afternoon, Mr. President, and thank you for this opportunity to talk to you.

A. Thank you, Colleen.

Q. Oh, I was wondering since the volunteer draft program isn't working too well that you'd put a draft system into effect, and if you would, would you draft women the same as men, as the Equal Rights Amendment infers?

A. Well, Colleen, we don't have any plans now to put in a draft system. So far we are still getting by with the voluntary armed forces. The major problem has been in the reserves. We are about 600, er, 800,000 people short, I believe now, in reserve recruitment. The regular armed forces are holding their own. But if I see it's necessary in the future to initiate a draft, then I would certainly recommend to the Congress that this be done. I would like to combine it with a much more comprehensive public service opportunity, where people might go into jobs like the Peace Corps or VISTA or teachers' aides, mental institutions, and so forth, along with military training as well. And I would make it much more all-inclusive than it has been in the past. I would not, for instance, exclude college students, and if it becomes necessary for national security, the likelihood is that women would be included as well. But I'd like to draw a distinction between military service and other service that would benefit our country just as much in a time of need or crisis. But I might re-emphasize that at this time we have no intention of going to a draft.

Q. O.K. Thank you.

Further Concern About Uganda
CALLER NO.27

MODERATOR: Thank you, Miss Muir. From Jerry Wildman, the next call, Mr. President. He's in Lake Worth, Florida.

Q. Good afternoon, Mr. President.

A. Good afternoon, Jay.

Q. Before I get to my question I would just like to add that I'm a candidate to the United State Naval Academy, and I hope to follow along in your footsteps. Now to my question. I would like to know what actions would be taken if any hostile acts would be taken against American or allied citizens living in Uganda.

A. O.K., that was a question early on the program, Jerry. I might just say that we had this question come up last weekend. We tried to handle it in a very unpublicized and careful way, knowing the unpredictability of Idi Amin, and I just let him know very forcefully and frankly that we were concerned about American citizens. And we also got other nations who have communications and the understanding better than we do, to deal with him and to help us there. I understand from the news that about eight or 10 different foreign leaders, mostly from the Moslem countries, contacted Amin. The West Germans helped us a great deal, and the crisis was averted. But I would guess that if this should recur in the future, and I hope it won't, that we'll handle it in the same way, Jerry.

Q. Oh, I see. Well, thank you very much, Mr. President.

Easing Burden of Health Costs
CALLER NO. 28

MODERATOR: Next question from Samuel Rankin of Billings, Montana, Mr. President.

Q. Good afternoon, Mr. President.

A. Good afternoon, Sam.

Q. I have a two-part question. The first is broken into two minor economic questions, and I hope that this has not been covered previously. If it has, maybe you would like to add some things that possibly you didn't get to add on the previous question.

I would like your commitment and your comments on a resolution in the public's favor that would alleviate the painfully high cost of medical care in the US And I know also that these two are related—a total commitment to the lowering of the transfer payments, which I believe are near forty-six percent of the income derived by the government from corporate and individual taxes.

A. Mr. Rankin, I don't know any way to answer your question very well at this point. I might say that these are two questions that we're working on simultaneously. The income tax changes are part of the transfer of payments. Also, the welfare system in its entirety needs to be reformed.

And by the first of May, Joe Califano who's the new Secretary of H.E.W., working with literally hundreds of different people, will come up for me and for the Congress with a comprehensive reform of the welfare system. It will be I would say next year before we can complete an adequate analysis of the health care system as a whole.

Now, we're trying now to hold down the cost of both medicine, treatment and also hospital care, but I can't answer your question yet.

Q. All right.

A. The first part of the answer, though, will be forthcoming May the first, with a welfare reform package, the second part, September 3, with income tax revision proposals. And the comprehensive health care would probably have to wait until next year. There's just so much we can do the first year, Sam.

Q. I appreciate that.

A. I'm sorry.

Q. And then the second part of my question, Mr. President. With many of our young people so involved in the past and presently with Vietnam, I would like to respectfully suggest that possibly you appoint a young person, preferably a Vietnam veteran, to accompany the mission headed for, or headed by Leonard Woodcock and including my state's most distinguished member in the Senate, Senator Mansfield, going to Vietnam in the near future. I believe this would help many of us, myself included, who felt hesitant in going to Vietnam and would now like to feel that we are helping rebuild that country.

And I respectfully request that my name be included on that list if and when you do decide to include a young member. And my wife wants me to be sure and say that if you're ever in Billings, Montana, that we would more than like to have you stay at our home.

A. Well, that's a nice invitation from you. My roommate at the Naval Academy back in ancient days was from Butte, Montana. His name was Blue Middleton, and I heard a lot about Montana from him. And of course, Senator Mike Mansfield is one of the most distinguished members of Congress that has ever served in our country.

The five members who will go to Vietnam have already been chosen. And Leonard Woodcock will be the chairman. As you said, Mike Mansfield will go. A woman, Marian Edelman, will also be on the trip. And a professional diplomat will go along. And also, one member of the House of Representatives as well. And, unfortunately, we won't have a veteran of the Vietnam War. I thought about this, Sam. And also, I thought about sending a member of an M.I.A. family.

Q. Right.

A. But my judgment was that we probably ought not to get people there who are so deeply and emotionally involved in the process. We've been encouraged so far—nobody can predict what's going to happen in the future—at the response of the Vietnamese government. And I think they want to reestablish relations with our own country.

They need help in exploring for oil, and in other ways. They need to trade with the outside world and not be completely dependent upon the Communist countries like China and Russia. And of course, we want to get an accounting for the more 2,500 Americans who still are not completely accounted for in Vietnam.

So, you have a good suggestion, but I've already chosen the five people, and they are now getting ready to go. They will arrive in Vietnam, if the plans go through, I think the sixteenth of March. So, it's well under way.

Q. Good, good. I think your proposal, your counterpoint to mine, was well taken and I can understand, you know, your thinking behind choosing someone that necessarily isn't.

MODERATOR: Thank you very much, Mr. Rankin. Thank you, sir, for calling. I'm going to suggest, Mr. President, that because we only have about 35 minutes left, that from here on out we ask the callers to limit themselves to one question. Or possibly a follow-up, if it's really necessary. But let's limit each caller to one subject matter at any rate.

CALLER No. 29

MODERATOR: The next caller, Mr. Louis Lawson of Richmond, Virginia. Mr. Lawson.

Q. Mr. Cronkite, President Carter: my name is Russell, you may call me Russell. Unfortunately, I had two questions before Mr. Cronkite had me limited to one, but I have one that is really uppermost in my mind.

I was wondering if you feel there's any inequity in passing laws which encourage the hiring of members of minority groups and women, while passing such laws implies resisting hiring equally qualified white males?

A: Yes, I don't like that concept either. I think that most of the laws that have been passed have been designed very narrowly to ensure that there is no continued discrimination against somebody because they are in a minority group or women.

Now the courts have interpreted this to mean that if a company, for instance, has historically excluded men and women from the labor force, for the old labor force, that they have to go back to take corrective action. But I think that all of the laws with which I am familiar, on equal employment opportunity, just guarantee that now and in the future there won't be discrimination and that if there has been a history of discrimination it will be corrected.

Q: I hope that's true. I've been unemployed for a while and I feel like I'm the victim of this kind of system. I want to say, though, before I go, that I'm really impressed by your desire to involve Americans more closely in the government, and I'm so pleased to have had the chance to talk to you. Thank you, President Carter.

A: Thank you. I might have to say that I've got a question we can answer, I think, from the man and his wife from Utah about the exclusion for disabled people. This was removed from the income tax law in the 1976 act—that is, sick pay exclusion for anyone except the permanently disabled. The Congress gave as its reason—and it sounded like a good reason—that such sick persons could deduct their medical expenses from the income tax and would therefore get a double benefit, and when anybody in our society, even if it is an afflicted person or disabled person, has a special exclusion, then other people have to pay the taxes for them. This is one of the things that will be assessed this year, and we may or may not put the double credit back for the permanently disabled, but my guess is that it would not be put back in.

Aid to Veterans Of Korean War
CALLER NO. 30

MODERATOR: The next caller. Mr. President, is Mrs. Cheryl Quinn of Cleveland, Ohio. Mrs. Quinn?

Q. Hello, Mr. President, I want to thank you for doing a great job and thank you for the inauguration ticket, and also my mom was in the Korean War and after she got out, she was signed up to get x-ray technician and she had to come up back to New York from Texas and then she got married and had kids and then [they] didn't give her what she wanted. They only gave her eight months of schooling and she has three years and some.

A. And you want to know what can be done about it, Cheryl, is that the question?

Q. Yes I do.

A. Well, she may have let her time run out on the G.I. Bill of Rights. That's probably what happened, the way you describe it. I don't think we can do anything about it. To be perfectly frank with you, without changing the law to make a special case for your mother and those like her, I doubt that it could be changed, Cheryl. When the law was written the Congress put into it that after a certain period of years—I think 10 years—that the G.I. benefits would be lost. But I'll have someone on my staff check out the case and see if there's something that can be done about it within the law itself. And they'll give you a call back this coming week. O.K.?

MODERATOR: Let me remind you that these calls are not being screened in any way for content. There's no censorship at all as the calls come into us here in the Oval Office of the White House.

Pay Increase For Congress
CALLER NO. 31

MODERATOR. Gerald Anderson, Denver, Colorado is the next caller.

Q. Mr. President.

A. Hi, Gerald.

Q. I'm wondering what is the justification with you trying to reduce the Federal budget—the justification behind the $12,000 pay increase to the Congress? How can you lower the budget by giving them $12,000 a year, and [give] us $50 back?

A. Gerald, that's a hard question for me to answer.

Q. That's why I thought I'd throw it at you.

A. I think you probably know that there is a law that was passed by Congress and the previous Presidents before I came into office that said that a commission would recommend pay levels for the Congress and for others like Federal judges and Cabinet officers, and unless the Congress voted no, that the pay raises would go into effect.

In other words, if the Congress does nothing, the pay raises go into effect. And that's what occurred. That law's been in the books for quite a while.

Q. All right. What I'm getting at, though, is with you trying to lower the budget why did you not try and do something to stop that if there was anything that could be done to stop it, why couldn't they some way be convinced that it was against, you know, the fiscal matters of the country to give them this increase?

A. Well, I might say that I think that the salary increases were justified. And one of the things that President Ford asked me to do before I was inaugurated, while he was still in office, was to add my support to the increase in salaries. I agreed not to object to the increase, provided there was a strict law on ethics tied to it, to limit the outside income of Congress members and to remove the conflicts of interest that exist between—with them—and also with people serving in the executive branch of Government.

I do think that the law ought to be changed, Gerald, to make sure that in the future if any sort of salary increase goes into effect that it not go into effect until after the following general election.

I think this would help a great deal to make all of us more careful about it, and it would mean that if Congress doesn't veto an increase that they would not get an increase in salary until after they had to face the voters again in the next general election.

With that change I would be in favor of continuing the law as it is.

Q. So there was no way that you could have stopped this increase?

A. That's correct. I didn't have any authority over it. But I have to say to you I could have made speeches around the country against it, but it was not my inclination to do so.

Q. Don't you feel that with the Congresspeople receiving this excessive amount of money compared to the average working person that it puts him out of touch with reality as far as what the average person has to go through to live in this country?

A. Well, I can't say that you're exactly right on that. No, I have seen from my own experience that it costs a member of Congress an enormous amount of extra money to maintain close contacts with the people back home, quite often to finance and to own a house, say, in Colorado where you live, and also to buy and to own or to rent an extremely expensive house here in Washington.

Also, the Congress member, in order to stay in office and to build up seniority to serve you and the other people around Denver better, has to run for office every two years.

Now there are some members of Congress who have no trouble raising money for a political campaign.

Others have to spend a lot of their own money in a political campaign. If you compare, say, a member of Congress who has to do that with a Federal judge who lives in Denver full time, who doesn't have to run for office, who gets the same amount of pay and who doesn't have the constant political world to live in and to deal with all kinds of complicated and very controversial questions like a Congressman does all in the open, I think that a Congressman deserves just as much salary as a Federal judge.

So, it cuts both ways and I think, Gerald, that in fairness to the members of Congress—I've never been in Congress, as you know—there are some extraordinary expenses that a member of Congress has that an average person, even a public servant like a Federal judge, does not have.

But I believe that one change that I described to you ought to be made and that is to let future salary increases go into effect only after the next general election.

MODERATOR. It is also true, Mr. President, isn't it, that the members of Congress, members of the Judiciary and the Executive Branch who are entitled to these raises, had not had one for a very long time and had fallen far behind the general cost-of-living increases.

A. I think the last raise went into effect about eight years ago.

I might say, Walter, that I made a mistake a while ago. I got my decimal point wrong on the shortage in the reserve figures because of not having a draft. The total reserve is about 800,000 and the shortage is about ten percent of that, 70,000 or 80,000. Somebody just called in and said that I said the shortage was 800,000 and I'm sorry I made that mistake.

MODERATOR. An officer in the reserve, I would guess.

A. I guess so.

CALLER NO. 32

MODERATOR. Sgt. David Cash of Miliani, Hawaii, is on the phone, Mr. President, our first call from the State of Hawaii. Sergeant Cash.

MODERATOR. . . . of Miliani, Hawaii, is on the phone, Mr. President, the first call from the State of Hawaii. Sergeant Cash.

Q. Good morning, Mr. President.

A. Good afternoon, Mr. Cash.

Q. I'm with the 25th Infantry Training Command and we have a Taekwondo program, which is a Korean martial art, and it's been with the 25th Infantry for the last three years, and we train Army personnel in it, you know, to be a better soldier in discipline and mental condition, and they turn out to be real better soldiers, real good soldiers, and I wonder how much difficult a problem, I mean, throughout the whole Army, United States Army, that we could have a program like that, establishing . . . infantry division?

MODERATOR: Do you understand what the program is, Mr. President, because I'm afraid I don't?

A. Could you tell me very briefly, Mr. Cash, Sergeant Cash, what the program is again?

Q. It's Taekwondo. It's a Korean martial art, like you have karate in Japan, in which we train the personnel which come in the division, as a . . .

A. I understand now. I think it's probably a good program to have, Sargent Cash. When I went through my own Navy training, I had the equivalent of karate training as part of my own preparation for military service. I might say that I broke my right collarbone in the process, but I recovered from it, and I think that the most severe kinds of physical training for combat soldiers is probably beneficial. It obviously ought to be done without abuse and without damage to the person, but I think that to be in top physical shape and know how to deal with personal hand-to-hand combat is a good thing. I hope I've understood your question properly.

Disagreement On Drug Use
CALLER NO. 33

MODERATOR: Thank you very much, Sargent Cash, and let's go to the next telephone call from Walter Lipman of Spring Valley in New York.

Q. Good afternoon, Mr. President.

A. Good afternoon.

Q. I'm rather amazed at being able to get a hold of you. This question is something that a bunch of friends of mine and I bandied back and forth and swore would never get on the air, but anyhow, Mr. President, it seems to—well, to me and my friends —that the term "drug addict" is more a function of one's social station than anything else.

Many famous people, such as Sigmund Freud, Sir Arthur

Conan Doyle, who wrote "Sherlock Holmes," and Dr. William Halstead, who was one of the founders of the Johns Hopkins Medical School, were quite heavy users of drugs such as cocaine and morphine, and yet were considered leaders of society in their day.

Now in this light, doesn't the prosecution of drug users and their habits by the Drug Enforcement Administration seem capricious, arbitrary and rather unjust?

A. No, it doesn't—well, not to me. I established a drug treatment program In Georgia while I was in office there as Governor. In July of 1972, I believe it was, we had eleven deaths in the Atlanta area from heroin overdose, primarily among young people. We put in a drug treatment program and kind of opened the whole question up to public awareness in October. And in the following twelve months, we had zero heroin deaths.

I've been in our treatment centers throughout the state of Georgia. In fact, my sons have worked in those treatment centers. And I've seen literally hundreds of young people's lives almost completely destroyed, by addiction to heroin in particular.

I think that a question like morphine would be a different one altogether. Morphine is a drug that's, as you know, administered legally—or as a previous caller said, a medication that's administered legally. But I would do all I can and am moving as aggressively as possible to stamp out the traffic in drugs like cocaine or heroin.

I believe they are a devastating affliction on our society and ought to be eliminated as much as we can.

Q. Mr. President, do you know the origin of the drug heroin?

A. Yes, I know it comes from poppies.

Q. No, but the purpose of it.

MODERATOR. Mr. Lipman, I thank you very much for your call but we're running a little short of time and we do want to get as many calls in as possible.

Offering Praise Over Pardon
CALLER NO. 34

MODERATOR. So we're going to move right along to Paul Guertin of Cudahy, Wisconsin.

Q. Mr. President?

A. Yes, Paul.

Q. One thing I have always wished I could tell you and now I have the chance, and that's pardoning the draft dodgers or evaders was one of the best things you could probably ever do because I feel that if somebody dodged the draft or was an objector of it, obviously they had a reason and they should be listened to, and forcing somebody to do something, even if they object to it or don't believe in it, is just taking away their rights.

MODERATOR: Do you have a question, Mr. Guertin, for the President.

Q. Not really. I just wanted to say that.

A. I might say that that was one of the most difficult decisions I made. I made my decision, though, quite early in the campaign. I never did mislead the American people about it. I made the major public announcement at the American Legion Convention out in the state of Washington last year—

one of the most critical audiences I could have had. I've just seen some public opinion poll results this week that showed that about forty-five percent of the American people thought I made a mistake, about forty-five percent of the American people thought I did the right thing and the other ten percent didn't have any opinion. So, there's no way to suit people. I feel that it's time for us to get over the Vietnam War as soon as we can, and I believe that those who have been excluded from living in our wonderful country for the last ten or twelve years have been punished pretty severely. So, I think that the deserters and all, as I said earlier on this program, ought to be handled on an individual case basis within the Department of Defense, and they are expediting their assessment of cases and will handle them under normal military and legal processes.

Q. It was really nice being able to talk to you. Thank you very much.

U.S. Restrictions on the Concorde
CALLER NO. 35

MODERATOR: The next call is from John-Raymond Lau of Yorktown Heights, New York.

Q. Mr. President?

A. Go right ahead.

Q. How are you doing, Mr. President?

A. Fine.

Q. I'd like to know what your opinion is of the French-English Concorde, and with the elections in France this week, do you feel that rejection of the Concorde would bring the power to the French Communist Party, and also, I'd like to say that many French citizens are counting on the SST to keep France from going the Communist way. So what is your opinion on that?

A: O.K. Our government has already expressed its opinion, Mr. Lau. The previous administration authorized the Concorde to come into our country for a fifteen-month trial period, and a couple of weeks ago I made a statement that I agreed with that decision and thought the Concorde ought to be given chance to fulfill its trial itself.

As you know, under the Federal law I have authority over Dulles Airport, and so did President Ford, and we're permitting the test flights to come into Dulles and we're very carefully monitoring the environmental consequences of the SST flights, including primarily noise.

Kennedy Airport in New York is not under my control at all. I have nothing to do with it, no authority over it. The New York Port Authority has that decision to make and I understand that on March tenth they are going to make a decision whether the Concorde can come in for test flights or not. I don't know what that decision will be.

I talked to President Giscard from France yesterday about the Concorde, and also talked to Governor Hugh Carey to let Governor Carey know, as President Giscard had asked me to, that the French people consider this a very important Issue.

My own statement to President Giscard is that we are not concerned about the SST flights because of commercial competition—about six years ago our own Congress decided not to go into the SST building business—and the whole problem in our country is noise and environmental quality maintenance.

Now, I might say one other thing. I think that the noise standards in our country are going to be stricter and stricter in the future and not more and more lenient, and the same noise standards ought to apply to an airplane whether it's a Concorde or a Lockheed or some other kind or any sort of American commercial plane, so I think we can establish strict environmental laws. I think they ought to apply to the SST flying a course at subsonic speeds and our own commercial planes the same.

But it's the environmental question that will exclude the Concorde if it is excluded, and not any sort of animosity toward the French people, nor is it any commercial competition between us and France on SST flights.

CALLER NO. 36

MODERATOR. Thank you, Mr. Lau. The next call is from Mrs. Runy Hewitt of San Bernardino, California.

Q. Yes. Good afternoon, President Carter.

A. Good afternoon, Mrs. Hewitt.

Q. Thank you for giving this time to the American people to speak with you; it is indeed a privilege we appreciate.

A. Thank you, ma'am.

Q. My question is why is it that veterans and Civil Service retirees are given two costs of living a year, but only one cost of living to Social Security retirees?

A. I don't know. I didn't realize that there was that difference, Mrs. Hewitt. That's the kind of question that I'm afraid I'll have to get an answer to, if there is an answer, and call you back about it Monday. I doubt if I'll have time to give the answer by the end of this program since we only have about 15 minutes to go. But I'll try to get the answer back to you.

Q. May I say that my brother's last wish was to be buried In Georgia, in Bluffton. Nolan Frisby. He was in the service there, and he's written me many letters about Georgia and how lovely it was.

A. Thank you very much.

Q. Beautiful people there.

A. Thank you so much. I might say that in Plains, which is a tiny little town, we have a Hewitt family. Maybe they'll tend to you and your brother.

Q. No, my name was Frisby before, and this is Nolan Frisby, he's passed away now, but his request was to be buried in Bluffton, where his family is now.

A. Oh, very good. Thank you, ma'am.

CALLER NO. 37

MODERATOR: Thank you, Mrs. Hewitt. John Caldwell of Atlanta, Georgia, is on the phone, Mr. President, and I'm advised he's 17 years old. Mr. Caldwell?

Q. Yes. Good afternoon, President Carter.

A. How're you doing?

Q. I'm 17 years old, and I'd like to know, do you plan to make any other place than Plains, Georgia your White House away from Washington?

A. No, sir. The only other place that I anticipate going on a fairly regular basis, as I mentioned early in the program, is to Camp David, which is a place for Presidents and has been used ever since Franklin Roosevelt was in office. But I don't intend to have several White Houses, as has been the case in the past.

Q. Thank you very much.

CALLER NO. 38

MODERATOR: Thank you, John Caldwell, and the next caller on the line is Ms. Leslie Pfenninger of Lanham, Maryland. Mr. President. Miss Pfenninger?

Q. Hello, President Carter, it's good to speak with you.

A. Thank you, Leslie.

Q. I'm a 1976 college graduate whose goal is to enter the Civil Service. And I've been working toward that goal since May. I might say it's a depressing effect to find the doors completely shut, and I'd like to know if the restrictions will be lifted to permit individuals like me to compete for jobs now only open to those currently in Civil Service or those of a reinstatable status.

A. Leslie, what is your profession or special training?

Q. I have a dual B.A. in psychology and sociology, and I also qualify as a statistician.

A. The best thing for me to do is to check on your particular case with the Civil Service and give you a call back this coming week about prospects for employment in the future, and I presume that the Civil Service has a record of your application, is that correct?

Q. Yes, sir, they do.

A. We'll be back in touch with you next week.

Q. Thank you, Mr. President. I hope you continue this kind of direct contact.

A. Good luck to you.

An Invitation To Minnesota
CALLER NO. 39

MODERATOR: I bet, Miss Pfenninger, when they told you the best way to get a job is just knock on a lot of doors, they didn't ever suggest telephoning the President on a national call-in show, but it seems to work. You're going to get an answer from him.

Les Wenz of Pittsburgh, Pennsylvania is on the phone, Mr. President.

Q. Good afternoon, Mr. President.

A. Russ, how are you doing?

Q. Very well. And I want to tell you you're doing wonderful, and I hope Congress keeps you going. I have a brief review and then a question.

President Calvin Coolidge came to Cannon Falls, Minnesota, on July 29, 1928, to dedicate the monument to Colonel William Caldwell, he was a Civil War hero. Last July the local American Legion post there suggested to the mayor that they issue a proclamation July 29 of each year as annual Presidents Day. And on this day, they're going to have a reaffirmation of our national unity problems, and what we could do and try in the rededication of our national ideals and that sort of thing.

The question, Mr. President, is: Would it be possible for you to accept an invitation from the Governor of Minnesota, or Mayor Geller of Cannon Falls to be the speaker at this national Presidents Day?

A. Mr. Wenz, I doubt it. This first year, I've tried to hold down as much as possible any public speaking on my part. I really need to learn more about this job, and as you know I've got a very good partner up here from Minnesota who might be available. I can't speak for him, but Fritz Mondale might be a possibility.

But I appreciate the invitation very much. If they would write me a letter, we can give then an official answer on it. And also, I appreciate the concept of reaffirming our patriotism in not only a national way, but also a local way, as you all have done.

Q. One of the things we'd like to do is remind everyone that a number of men in their prime of life gave up their life or were injured seriously, you know; that that's why we have our freedom and independence.

A. Good luck to you.

Q. Thank you.

CALLER NO. 40

MODERATOR. Thank you, Mr. Wenz. And your next caller, Mr. President, is Mr. Kerry Kimble of Fulton, Missouri. Mr. Kimble.

Q. Yes, Mr. President, my question covers the War Powers Resolution. Do you feel that it infringes upon your power as Commander in Chief in the limiting or getting the approval from Congress to continue the use of American forces in a certain situation past the sixty days?

A. Mr. Kimble, it is a reduction obviously in the authority that the President has had prior to the Vietnam War, but I think it's an appropriate reduction. My own attitude toward government is that I would never see our nation approach a time of war with any sort of predictability about it without discussing it thoroughly and frequently with the Congress and also letting the American people know what is going on.

And although we did get involved in the Vietnam War and even fought extensively in Cambodia without telling the American people and sometimes lying to them, I would never have that inclination.

So, I have no hesitancy about communicating with Congress, consulting with them and also letting the American people know what we do before we start any combat operation.

And I think with that process we can minimize greatly the chances that we will get involved in combat anywhere in the world.

Q. Sir, would you accept their approval for your action on that?

A. Yes. There is, I think there is, I think, a provision that in a time of crisis where an unanticipated attack might be launched against our country's security that I could act. But to continue any sort of military operation I would have to get the Congress's approval and I have no doubt that that's the right thing to do.

Negotiations With Panama
CALLER NO. 41

MODERATOR: Thank you, Mr. Kimble. Thank you, and the next call is from Mr. Johnny Strickland, Fayetteville, North Carolina.

Q. Good afternoon, Mr. President. This is Johnny Strickland from Fayetteville, North Carolina. I want to thank you for this opportunity to talk with you, and I would like to know what your sentiments are on the Panama Canal 1904 treaty and changing it.

A. O.K. It's good to hear from you, Mr. Strickland. My sister lives in Fayetteville, as you may know, and I am glad to answer your question. We are now negotiating with Panama as effectively as we can. As you may or may not know, the treaty signed when Theodore Roosevelt was President gave Panama sovereignty over the Panama Canal Zone itself. It gave us control over the Panama Canal Zone, as though we had sovereignty. So we've always had a legal sharing of responsibility over the Panama Canal Zone. As far as sovereignty is concerned, I don't have any hang-up about that. I would hope and expect that after the year 2000 that we would have an assured capacity or capability of our country with Panama guaranteeing that the Panama Canal would be open and of use to our own nation and to other countries. So that's the subject of the negotiation now—it has been going quite a while—is to phase out our military operations in the Panama Canal Zone, but to guarantee that even after the year 2000 that we would still be able to keep the Panama Canal open to the use of American and other ships.

Q. I understand, and I certainly hope that we are not too lenient, because we have lots of money invested in the Canal Zone and I really think the Canal Zone belongs to us, a whole lot more than most people think it does.

Public School Commitment
CALLER NO. 42

MODERATOR. Thank you, Mr. Strickland, and the next call comes from Miss Michelle Stanley of North Benton, Ohio, and Mr. President, Miss Stanley is 11 years old.

Q. Jimmy? Hi, I just had to thank you for sending me the inauguration—to your inauguration.

A. Did you get a chance to come?

Q. No, I didn't, but I was just happy to get it. But I have another question. Why doesn't Amy go to a private school?

A. Well, I hope sometimes, Michelle, you could come and visit with Amy. She goes to the public school and did in Georgia, when we lived there as well. She enjoys it very much and I have a very strong commitment to the public school system and don't have anything against the private school system, but I think it helps the public schools in Washington, D.C., to have the President's daughter go there. And it indicates to other parents that I have confidence in the public school system all over the country. Amy goes to school with children, I think, from twenty-six foreign nations as well as from our own country. And so far she likes the school very much. So, because of my commitment to the public school and because Amy likes it, those are the reasons, Michelle. Good luck to you.

I might say, Walter, that I've got an answer to Mrs. John Ritchey's question about the payment for the Ottawa Indian lands. This bill has already been signed into law and there's $10.2 million to be distributed to members of the Ottawa tribe. The Department of Interior is right now writing rules for the distribution of the funds, and by late summer of this year, the money will be distributed. So that ought to be good news for Mrs. John Ritchey of Georgetown, Kentucky.

MODERATOR: Mr. President, you got the answer there for her just in time because we have just about run out of time. I'm just curious, Mr. President, before we close this off today, what you thought of the questions you got to this first experiment in meeting the people through the telephone call-in broadcast.

A. Walter, I liked it. The questions that come in from people all over the country are the kind that you would never get in a press conference—the news people would never raise, like the Ottawa Indian question. And I think it's very good for me to understand directly from the American people what they are concerned about and questions that have never been asked of me and reported through the news media, so my inclination would be to do this again in the future, and I'll wait and see how the American people react to it to see whether or not I've done a good job to make it worth their while.

But I want to thank you for being here with me this afternoon. The two hours passed very quickly, and I've enjoyed it and learned a lot from it.

MODERATOR: I think it is indeed, and we'd be glad to sign you again, Mr. President.

A. Good deal.

MODERATOR: We have run out of time. We thank you for your time and the cooperation of your entire staff in making this broadcast possible. We regret such a small number of those who wanted to talk with you actually did get to call in and from many of you who did call in and didn't get through to the President, we apologize for that. A special thanks to all of you who are interested in this new broadcast idea, and from President Carter and me in the Oval Office of the White House, good afternoon.

I'm Walter Cronkite, CBS News.

ACKNOWLEDGMENTS

In writing of these *Journeys*, I have been graced by two superb partners. From the first word to the last, the Managing Editor, my spouse, Karen A.B. Jagoda, turned jangles into sentences, paragraphs and chapters.

Developmental Editor, Ken Keuffel, a former newspaper reporter, enhanced the depth, coherence and accuracy of the manuscript through his many probing questions, and by suggesting that I work from an outline.

An early reader was my trusted friend, Richard L. Cohen, whose suggestion that the original manuscript needed more "meat" resulted in additional focus on how each of us can make a difference in the 2020 election.

Michael Ebeling, Ebeling & Associates Literary Agency, was one of many agents who encouraged this project, but only Michael suggested a practical way forward by putting me in touch with John Koehler.

This writer is fortunate to have as his Publisher the solid John Koehler. John's kind, engaging demeanor matches perfectly with his partner, Joe Coccaro, the sensitive, experienced Executive Editor for Koehler Books. I lucked out when Joe turned the manuscript over for word-by-word editing by Elizabeth Marshall McClure, an exceptional professional. The book was brought together most agreeably by Design Director, Kellie Emery.

I add sincerely that errors of fact are completely my own responsibility.

BIBLIOGRAPHY

Associated Press, *Stylebook and Briefing on Media Law,* Perseus Publishing, 2012

Beck, Jay *Casting Stones: 1985 Election in Greece,* Mindstir Media, 2018

Bernstein, Carl and Woodward, Bob, *All The President's Men,* Simon and Schuster, 1974

Blackburn, Dr. Elizabeth and Epel, Dr. Elissa, *The Telomere Effect: A Revolutionary Approach to Living Younger, Healthier, Longer,* Grand Central Publishing, 2018

Blumenthal, Sidney, *The Permanent Campaign,* Beacon Press, 1980

Boller, Paul F., Jr., *Presidential Campaigns,* Oxford University Press, 1984

Bramer, William Lee, *The Gay Place,* University of Texas Press, 1995

Brinkley, Douglas, The Unfinished Presidency, Jimmy Carter's Journey to the Nobel Prize, Penguin Books, 2005

Carter, Jimmy, *Keeping Faith: Memoirs of A President,* Bantam Books, 1982

Carter, Jimmy, *Palestine Peace Not Apartheid,* Simon & Schuster, 2007

Carter, Jimmy, *Why Not The Best,* Broadman Press, 1975

The Chicago Manual of Style, The University of Chicago Press, 2017

Constitution of the United States, American Civil Liberties Union, New York, 2005

Diamond, Jared, *Guns, Germs and Steel: The Fates of Human Societies,* W.W. Norton & Company, 2017

Eizenstat, Stuart, *President Carter, The White House Years*, St. Martin's Press, 2018

Evans, Eli N., *The Provincials,* Atheneum, 1973

Frankel, Max, *The Times of My Life*, Random House, 1999

Friedlander, Saul, *Nazi Germany and the Jews, 1933-1945*, Harper Perennial, 2009

Friendly, Fred W., *Due to Circumstances Beyond Our Control,* Random House, 1967

Goetzmann, William H., *Exploration and Empire*, Alfred A. Knopf, 1971

Handlin, Oscar, *The Uprooted*, University of Pennsylvania Press, 2002

Harari, Yuval Noah, *Sapiens: A Brief History of Humankind,* Harper Perennial, 2018

Herzberg, Don, *Dancing on Earth: Poems*, Magic Begonia Press, 2019

Jagoda, Barry, *Gulf of Tonkin Resolution,* Columbia University, 1967

Jagoda, Karen A. B., *Crossing the River: The Coming of Age of the Internet in Politics and Advocacy*, Xlibris, 2005

Jagoda, Karen A. B., *About Face: The Dramatic Impact of the Internet on Politics and Advocacy,* E-Voter Institute Press, 2009

Jordan, Hamilton, *Crisis: The Last Year of the Carter Presidency,* Putnam, 1982

Kraus, Sidney, *The Great Debates: Carter vs. Ford, 1976,* Indiana University Press, 1979

Kuhn, Thomas, Structure of Scientific Revolutions, 1962, University of Chicago Press

Maraniss, David, *A Good Family,* Simon & Schuster, 2019

McGarr, Kathryn J., *The Whole Damn Deal: Robert Strauss and the Art of Politics*, Public Affairs, 2011

Morris, Willie, *North Toward Home,* Houghton Mifflin, 1967

Neustadt, Richard E., *Presidential Power*, Free Press, 1991

Popkin, Samuel, *The Reasoning Voter: Communication and Persuasion in Presidential Campaigns*, University of Chicago Press, 1994

Powell, Jody, *The Other Side of The Story,* William Morrow, 1984

Quinn, Sally, *We're Going to Make You a Star*, Simon and Schuster, 1975

Robinson, Michael J., *Over the Wire and on TV: CBS and UPI in Campaign '80*, Russell Sage Foundation, 1984

Rosenbloom, David Lee, *The Election Men,* Quadrangle Books, 1973

Schram, Martin, *Running for President, 1976,* Stein and Day, 1977

Talese, Gay, *The Kingdom and the Power: Behind the Scenes at The New York Times: The Institution That Influences the World,* Random House, 1966

Talese, Gay and Lichtner, Marvin, *New York: a Serendipiter's Journey,* Harper, 1961

Walker, Matthew, *Why We Sleep,* Simon and Schuster, 2017

White, Theodore H., *America in Search of Itself: The Making of the President, 1956-1980*, Harper & Row, 1982

White, Theodore H., *The Making of the President, 1960-1972*, Harper & Row, 1960-1973

Winfrey, Carey, *Starts and Finishes,* E.P. Dutton, 1972

Witty, Joanne, *Brooklyn Bridge Park*, Fordham University Press, 2016

INDEX